Leadership Scaffolding

INSTITUTE OF LEADERSHIP & MANAGEMENT (ILM)
THE PROFESSIONAL INSTITUTE OF CHOICE FOR TODAY'S MANAGER

Founded over 50 years ago and now part of the City & Guilds Group, the Institute of Leadership & Management (ILM) is unique among professional bodies. As the largest awarding body for management – related qualifications with over 75,000 candidates each year, the ILM recognises and fosters good management practice. As a professional body, ILM also offers informal personal and professional support to practising leaders and managers across all disciplines and at every career stage.

20,000 members have already found that ILM membership gives them the strategic, ongoing support they need to fulfil their aims, enabling them to enhance their skills, add to their professional expertise and to develop a wider network of valuable business contacts.

For further information on becoming a member of ILM please contact the Membership Department on telephone + 44 (0) 1543 251 346. www.i-l-m.com

Leadership Scaffolding

JUDITH ELLIOTT

Chandos Publishing
Oxford · England

Published in association with

Institute of Leadership
& Management

Chandos Publishing (Oxford) Limited
Chandos House
5 & 6 Steadys Lane
Stanton Harcourt
Oxford OX29 5RL
UK
Tel: +44 (0) 1865 884447 Fax: +44 (0) 1865 884448
Email: info@chandospublishing.com
www.chandospublishing.com

First published in Great Britain in 2006

ISBN:
1 84334 205 7 (paperback)
1 84334 206 5 (hardback)
978 1 84334 205 2 (paperback)
978 1 84334 206 9 (hardback)

British Library Cataloguing-in-Publication Data.
A catalogue record for this book is available from the British Library.

Typeset by Domex e-Data Pvt. Ltd.
Printed in the UK and USA.

Only connect ... live in fragments no longer
EM Forster, Howard's End

Contents

Acknowledgements   *ix*

List of figures   *xi*

List of tables   *xiii*

Preface   *xv*

About the author   *xxi*

1   Quoting for the job (get your aim straight)   **1**

     Defining vision and purpose   2

     Establish your accountabilities   10

     The way we do things round here (values)   14

     Create your own business plan   18

     Scaffolding summary   23

2   Beginning the scaffolding frame (information processes)   **25**

     Get your scaffolding assembled   27

     Step 1: Micro-strategy   28

     Step 2: Operational plans   34

     Step 3: Information flow   38

     Step 4: Knowledge management   43

     Step 5: Networking   46

     Step 6: Glue   48

3   The scaffolders (off on the right foot)   **53**

     Step 1: Job role and accountabilities   55

     Step 2: Agreeing objectives   59

Step 3: Setting performance standards 63

Step 4: Providing resources 64

Step 5: Recruitment processes 65

Scaffolding summary 76

4   Climbing the scaffolding (meetings and recognition) 79

The basic rules for meetings 79

Involvement and empowerment 86

Scaffolding summary 95

5   Feedback on the construction (monitor and review
people's progress) 97

Step 1: Monitoring work 97

Step 2: Assess the data you collect 99

Step 3: Providing feedback 101

Step 4: Dealing with underperformance 109

Scaffolding summary 110

6   Improving the structure (help people develop) 113

Step 1: Start with the strategy 114

Step 2: Team and individual plans 117

Step 3: Development solutions 127

Step 4: Evaluation 127

Scaffolding summary 132

7   Review the structure 133

The golden truths 133

Audit yourself 134

Final skills tips 143

Bibliography 147

Index 151

Acknowledgements

For my father, who said I would have to write this book three times to get it anywhere near acceptable, and he was right.

Many people helped with this book and in different ways. First, thank you to the following for their patience and good sense when discussing their views on what makes a good middle manager: Kate Carrick, Liz Wilson, Paul Bowden, Paul Cooke, Bill Parsons, and Ann Wilson. Thank you to all my clients, past and present, who provide regular material. Thank you to Julia for her technical expertise with the PC and also her general support and encouragement and thank you to Sonia for listening, support and many coffees.

Finally thank you to Jim and Sophie for putting up with a virgin writer, and Jim especially for being on my side all the time.

List of figures

1.1 One-year business plan for department x   21

2.1 Pyramid strategy model with specifics towards
the top and broader visions at the bottom   29

2.2 Four strategy pillars   30

2.3 Simple strategy template   31

2.4 The Eight-Stage Communication Circle
(Icke, 2003)   38

2.5 The DIKAR model (Venkataram, 1996)   44

2.6 Visually mapping network links   48

3.1 The Performance Management Cycle
(Drucker 1958)   55

3.2 Applying the McKinsey 7-S model to an
individual in your department   58

3.3 Shortlisting matrix with weighting   70

5.1 A simple, generic view of performance reviews   105

6.1 Why develop the workforce   115

6.2 The development gap   115

List of tables

1.1 Questions to ask, and why   6

1.2 McKinsey 7-S (Peters et al., 1980)   13

3.1 Interview structure: a recommended pattern
     (Torrington and Hall, 1991)   75

6.1 Where to collect data and for what   119

6.2 Comparing development methods   128

6.3 Key evaluation questions   130

6.4 Hamblin's evaluation levels   131

Preface

There are a lot of good books and courses around on management. They all tell you *what* you need to know to do a decent job as a middle manager. This one is different because it's the first one to tell you *how to*. Not just how to delegate, or motivate, or write a strategy, but how to do it all. And how to do it all so that everything joins up, seamlessly.

Successful organisations actually put a range of processes in place to enable managers to manage. They set up a framework, if you like, to work by – mechanisms that encourage managers to delegate, motivate, involve and so on.

I call this *scaffolding*. Different organisations have their own, unique scaffolding, which is fine. Pizza meetings for the whole company on a Friday afternoon work well in some places, not in others. A state of the nation address from the MD is pretty common but the style varies hugely. Each to his own.

But in the following chapters we will review the minimum scaffolding required. The bad news for some of you is that the minimum is actually a lot. But simple though.

Of course, you might be a pretty darn good manager, in a pretty well-scaffolded organisation. In that case, regard this book as a sort of pulse check. I interviewed a fair bunch of seriously good managers for this book and every single one of them found at least one process that we talked about that needed improving in their area.

On the other hand, you might work in a place that is distinctly short on scaffolding. You might even take an active dislike to some of it. 'Write a micro-strategy ... but why?' I hear you say. Or, 'meetings, more meetings!'.

Trust me, I get around quite a bit. The truly excellent middle managers have a full range of processes in place, regardless of what the rest of the organisation does. And not only do they have the range, but the scaffolding is joined up; there are no gaps.

The other two significant keys to their success are:

1. *Tenacity* – they set up the processes and they pursue them consistently, year in year out.

2. *Involvement* – they use the processes to involve their teams. They consult, seek ideas, encourage creativity, delegate; the whole shooting match.

Perhaps, now you are aware of this concept of scaffolding, it is time to tell you about the processes. Each chapter describes the steps you take to achieve certain outcomes. Each of these steps are the scaffolding, to be taken year in, year out.

Don't be put off, it isn't rocket science, anyone can do it. It's just that a lot of managers don't.

The words look fancy, very corporate, but the actions are simple – and so are the results. The overall scaffolding, when you stand back to admire it, will look complex, but we all know each piece of scaffolding is just a straight piece of metal, and not that long either.

The following bullet points give an overview of the forthcoming chapters – of both the scaffolding processes and the outcomes:

- **Chapter 1**

  Scaffolding processes to: Define organisational vision, values and your own accountability

  Outcomes: Department business plan to give direction

- **Chapter 2**

  Scaffolding processes to: Manage information flow and knowledge

  Outcomes: Department micro-strategy to achieve results

  Department operational plan to schedule and monitor work

  Effective use of knowledge

- **Chapter 3**

  Scaffolding processes to: Agree individual accountabilities, performance objectives, work standards, resources and recruitment

  Outcomes: Clear direction for every individual in the team

- **Chapter 4**

  Scaffolding processes to: Set up a robust meeting framework

  Recognise team and individual efforts

  Outcomes: The best meeting system to allow effective communication

  Simple recognition that makes people feel good

- **Chapter 5**

  Scaffolding processes to: Monitor and feedback on progress

  Outcomes: Effective feedback which improves performance

- Chapter 6

  Scaffolding processes to: Develop skills, knowledge and attitude

  Outcomes: Team and individual development plans to move people forward

- Chapter 7

  Scaffolding processes to: Check it's all working

  Outcomes: Continuous improvement

In every chapter, alongside the steps to take are nuggets of advice (skills tips). These are the words of wisdom, very rarely written down, about how to behave. Not often covered on courses or in management books, these golden rules are known by the truly good managers. Well worth sticking to.

Just to get you in the right frame of mind, I have compiled a series of quotes on the attributes and behaviours that senior managers believe about middle managers. It is not a definitive list but it does set the tone of the book quite well.

What makes a really good middle manager?

- 'Positive, keen. In some ways, a blind optimist, at least perceived that way.'

- 'Not overly empathetic with the staff, they never go native but are in tune with, and an advocate for, their people.'

- 'Positive managers always seem to get more done than the negative ones.'

- 'The positive managers are taken seriously when they criticise because they always put up solutions to problems.'

- 'They think like senior managers and have a good all round understanding of the business.'

- 'They look off their own radar.'

- 'They deal with other people's negativity.'

- 'The good ones come to me with ideas or proposals. They challenge me.'

- 'The good ones use the communication framework to its full advantage, which means to their own advantage as well as the organisation's.'

Before we get started, we should just take a brief look at leadership style. Are you *autocratic* (a bit of a dictator to say the least), *consultative* (firm on direction, but actually listen to your team), or *empowering* (hand on the tiller, but set the team up to manage themselves)?

Most training courses and books in the last 20 years push us towards the empowering or at least consultative style in the belief that the autocratic leader has had his/her day in business. In my experience, though, there are still a lot of dictators out there.

Whichever style you have, or choose to aspire to, all I ask is that you consider the effect on others. By all means be a dictator, but don't be surprised if people clam up or clash with you, just pick your team members appropriately. By the same token, if you choose to consult, then make sure you actually act on the team's ideas. And finally empower, but be prepared to put time and effort into supporting the team – don't just abdicate.

Get some feedback on your style before you read this book. Adjust as you see fit, and then put your scaffolding up to suit.

About the author

Judith Elliott is the Managing Director of elconsulting Cambridge Limited and a Fellow of the Chartered Institute of Personnel and Development.

For the last 13 years Judith has worked with clients to solve people issues such as communication, performance management, and team working. Judith's principal strength is her ability to 'walk in the client's shoes'. By working alongside, getting to grips with the combination of culture and business goals, and challenging thinking along the way, she supports management teams in finding integrated solutions to the people side of the business.

She, and her team, coach top teams and also deliver Institute of Leadership and Management (ILM) accredited management development programmes.

Before starting elconsulting Judith had a 15-year management career in retailing when she had direct responsibility for large teams of people and successful commercial results. This sharp-end leadership experience, building effective teams to achieve multi-million pound turnovers, gave Judith the ability to think strategically but at the same time convert business plans into team actions.

She has worked closely with top teams from a range of organisations including Bosch Rexroth, Eversheds, Bluestone, Cambridge University, Domino Printing Sciences, Huntingdon District Council and many SMEs. She also lectures on the CIPD Certificate in Personnel Practice programme.

The author may be contacted at:

elconsulting Cambridge Limited
St John's Innovation Centre
Cowley Road, Cambridge, CB4 OWS

E-mail: *Judith@elconsulting.co.uk*

Quoting for the job
(get your aim straight)

This chapter is wholly focused on establishing the shape of the building around which you will be erecting scaffolding, because it is essential to get your ducks in a row before selecting your scaffolding. So find out, as best you can, the organisation's purpose and plans. For some of you that's going to be easy, for the rest it will simply require detective work and some intelligent questions.

Most books on management start at chapter one with establishing *The Vision* and this book is no different. It is, after all, one of the simple truths – if you don't know where you are going how will you plan how to get there?

After establishing direction, you need to find out where senior managers will hold you personally accountable. So this chapter concerns itself with:

- *Organisational vision*: where are we going, what are we trying to be?

- *Your accountability*: where your responsibility begins and ends; often never articulated but nevertheless known by senior managers so it's important to know what they are thinking.

- *The organisation's values*: every organisation has a set, written down or not, so best you know what they are.

- *Your very own business plan*: regardless of how woolly or robust the organisational plan, you need your own, basically for the sake of your own efficiency and effectiveness.

Don't fret, it's not rocket science, just good detective work – though admittedly more Inspector Morse than The Bill.

Defining vision and purpose

Your organisation may very well have an all-singing, all-dancing vision but, quite frankly, I would be surprised if they do. Most visions are either woolly or simply proclaim that the company wants to be the best in class. Well, don't we all?

Unfortunately this must be your starting point, because if you do not know, quite clearly and concisely, where your organisation is heading then how will your team know? Everything you all do on a daily basis hinges on this vision if you are to be successful, or at least have a chance at success.

A good example of the effects of an absence of vision comes from an interesting conversation I had with a team of middle managers from a world-class academic establishment. The managers were not academics, but ran all the services to keep the establishment going, as well as offering fairly sophisticated conference facilities to generate income. Although the academics believed they were in the premier league, the managers led a wholly reactive existence because they had no idea what sort of service level they were trying to offer. Maybe that was acceptable for one client group, the academics themselves, and only maybe, but for the conference trade it led to a mixed offering – quality food and surroundings but poor service.

'So what level of service do you want to offer?' I asked.

'What we can, given the staff we have.' They said.

'But what will make you different from all the other conference facilities nearby?'

'Oh, we have lovely buildings.'

'So do the others. What's stopping you being world-class, like the academics?'

'Oh, we couldn't compete with high-class conference facilities.'

'Why not? You have a world-class venue. Look, do you want to be a Woolworths or a Harvey Nichols? – Pick 'n' mix or classy?'

'Definitely Harvey Nichols.'

In the end, they jointly decided to be premier league for day conferences with the unique selling point of friendly service, (as opposed to pompous, for which their competitors were famous). From there they worked out the type of client that would use them, how they would secure repeat business and finally, but most significantly, how they could increase profit. All this instead of running around like headless chickens, trying to be all things to all clients and falling at most fences.

Now is the time to look at a good, robust vision that clearly does what it says on the tin. Professor Hugh Davidson (2002) researched 125 of the world's major companies and institutions to find the best purpose, vision and values. He describes, 'The best company in the investment-banking sector I met was Goldman Sachs'.

- *Purpose*: To provide excellent investment and development advice to major companies.
- *Vision*: To be the world's premier investment bank in every sector.

Every word counts ... They're just in the investment, development and advice business and only operate with the Fortune 500. If you're not a Fortune 500 they're very unlikely to be interested in talking to you. So that's what they're here for. Their vision is to be the world's premier investment bank in every sector in which they operate. That's a continuing vision and a pretty hard one to keep on achieving year in year out. (Davidson 2002)

For the sake of clarity we will use Professor Davidson's definitions for words like *purpose*, *mission* and *values*; different organisations use these words in different ways but his research gathered some common themes.

- *Purpose*: What are we here for? In other words 'mission' but this word has fallen from grace in the business world, because many such statements sound good but don't really mean much.
- *Vision*: What is our long-term destination? Looking ahead for 5, 10, 20 years.
- *Values*: Beliefs and behaviours to guide us on the journey.

So the first set of questions you need to ask are all around the vision and purpose (values we will cover later). You might be lucky and find your organisation is one of the few with a robust vision, but of the companies Davidson researched, he found only 34 per cent of them to have strong visions.

It is therefore more likely that you will find a weak vision which more or less says, 'We want to be the best at what we do' or words to that effect. Or maybe there will be nothing written down at all.

The detective work

- Step 1: Ask your immediate line manager the questions in Table 1.1.
- Step 2: Ask another director/senior manager (optional).
- Step 3: Ask your managing director.

Who you ask much depends on the prevailing management structure and how robust the written vision. Clearly some MDs are out of reach or would expect the vision to be robust enough for your line manager to be more than able to interpret. Whatever the accessibility, it is worth getting as high up the food chain as you can, because you are not going to ask just the obvious questions, and most MDs, in my experience, love talking about their babies (i.e. their organisations).

Just take care in your preparation; the questions need to sound intelligent in themselves, and you need to sound as if you have put some thought already into the whole thing. Going in with a blank piece of paper will make you appear daft.

So the opener from you would be along the lines of, 'I need to get a clear idea/be sure in my own mind exactly what this organisation wants to achieve. Do you have some time to set aside for this? It won't take more than 30 minutes'. (It might, but that's up to them – when managing directors especially start talking about their baby they tend to get carried away.)

'Yes but, no but...' I hear you say. 'I've been in the organisation five years – I can't bowl in and ask *now*!' Oh yes you can – just put a different spin on your request for time. Perhaps by saying 'I want to put together a plan for my department for the next year. Could you spare me an hour to talk through the organisational strategy first?'

Table 1.1 Questions to ask, and why

Ask questions to gather information on...	The purpose of the question
Organisational history	Find out the key factors for growth or change of direction.
Current state of the market you are in	Competitors activity (up and down). Other external influences.
Key stakeholders	Always interesting to know who senior managers believe are the key stakeholders after customers. Often find who controls the purse strings here.
Target market	This can be surprisingly difficult for some MDs, especially those who want to sell everything they have to anybody who will buy.
Key type of customer	Who are they, what do they want to buy as opposed to what have we got to sell?
Most profitable products/services	Cut to the chase – where do we make money? Another tricky question for some so ask for hard data here, not best guesses.
Weaknesses in the organisation	Where does the MD think we are weak? Important to know their perceptions as well as their facts.
What growth is planned?	A key question, slipped in the middle, but tells you exactly what is on the horizon. MDs with no clear vision or strategy will give you only financials here, the rest will give more detail.
Are we going for profit or turnover?	Yes to both, although common, is not good enough; you want to know where the growth is expected – have you got to batten down the hatches and improve profit or go hell for leather to grow turnover? Are we building on the existing customer base or adding more?
Quality	Are we going for top-end, high-quality or volume?
Cost control	How far does cost control go? Can I make business cases for expenditure? How are the budgets put together?

Table 1.1	Questions to ask, and why (*cont'd*)

Ask questions to gather information on...	The purpose of the question
People	What is the situation on recruitment, staffing levels, 'growing our own'? What shape is the reward system (as in pay)?
Values	How do we do things round here?
Organisational strategy	Either get a document outlining the business strategy for the next 1–3 years, or maybe copies of slides from the last 'state of the nation' address from the MD to the people, or a series of coherent/ incoherent verbal ideas.

They will be surprised, and possibly on the back foot with either of these requests so give them thinking time and therefore a heads-up on what you want to ask.

Once you have their attention, one way to start would be 'My understanding, from the research I have done, is this ... Is that how you see it?'

You will notice that the questions you need to ask go far deeper than simply purpose and vision. We need to research such issues as history, the market, the future, strategies and so on. The past always affects the future, and you need to know, for sure, the influences on senior managers so that you can get into their particular groove. The conversation should result in you being quite clear about where the organisation is going and why. You might also notice that strategy is last on the list. That's not to say it's the least important – far from it – that is what you are after, but you want to shape the conversation to get the background first. However, if the MD starts with strategy, then let him, just don't accept only that. I am well aware that like visions, strategies come in all shapes and sizes. Your particular organisation may very well have a fairly reasonable strategy, even though it has no articulated vision but you still need to be acquainted with the influences, in order to be able to design your own (covered in Chapter 2 – so pace yourself).

Before you ask for a meeting, carry out your own analysis of the organisation, as you perceive it. This gives you the basis of a better quality discussion and shows that you have done some homework. You might even pick up some points that others had put on the back burner or not even considered lately.

Quick analysis

There are choices to be made here, from other books you can buy, but we should just stick to the simple, tried and tested: PESTLE and SWOT. The first gives you an insight into external pressures on the organisation, the second is a simple navel gazing tool, i.e. a snapshot analysis of the organisation's current position. Both of these together will give you sufficient insight to frame intelligent questions for the business conversations with both line manager and MD. You might even want to show the MD your SWOT analysis, under the guise of asking him to fill in the blanks. It shows that you have done some homework but you are very interested in his beliefs – both flattering and intelligent. It's what they commonly call these days a 'no-brainer'.

Don't waste too much time allocating issues under the correct heading; it's enough that you have a good quality list of influences that affect your organisation. I have had managers in the past who say that their organisation is not really ever affected by external pressures. That is piffle – every organisation has external pressures, to a greater or lesser degree.

- *Political interventions*: Would a change in government affect you? European or global political issues?

- *Economic changes*: Regional or national. Boom and bust or steady as we go? Bubbles bursting and interest rate changes.

- *Social trends*: Fashion and fad. New trends.

- *Technological innovation*: Either in processes or products. Internet, wireless, software etc.

- *Legal*: New laws: company and employment. Laws changing the way you work.

- *Environmental*: Pollution, waste control, the ozone and so on.

SWOT analysis

- Strengths
- Weaknesses
- Opportunities
- Threats

Consider the following points and decide whether they are strengths, weaknesses, opportunities or threats. Generally speaking the strengths lead to opportunities, and so can be made into targets. Weaknesses lead to threats, and therefore issues to be dealt with.

- Financial position
- Skills levels of workforce
- Company brand recognition (local, national, global)
- State of machinery in use
- Ownership of premises

- Location of business e.g. transport links
- State of the competition
- Stock/supply situation
- Wastage situation
- New products
- New/old technology
- Cost of staff
- Ability to expand
- Interest rates
- Seasonal demands

Skills tips

- Allow the senior manager to pick their best time for the conversation; nobody likes to get caught on the back foot.
- Do not be fobbed off by being given a business plan to read instead of a conversation. Read the business plan and base questions on the key aspects but always ask questions eye to eye.
- Listen for underlying messages or unspoken concerns – watch their faces. Probe deeper but do not push.
- No-one likes a tree shaker, the sort that asks too many difficult questions and appears to be too challenging. So stay pleasant and calm, laugh at their jokes, and keep it light!

Establish your accountabilities

After all that interrogation, you should have a clear idea of what the organisation is aiming for, so the next step is to establish exactly what *you* are accountable for. Not your objectives, they come later, but what you will be seen to be responsible for, and that is always wider than specific results or tasks. Try to think of accountability under a set of all encompassing headings. You could design your own, or base the headings on your organisation's strategy (as long as that is all encompassing) or you could use an established model. One successful, high-tech organisation I know uses the McKinsey 7-S, another type uses the Balanced Scorecard. Both are outlined below.

I suggest you carry out a dummy run at home with a large drink in your hand, and make a stab at defining your own accountabilities, as you perceive them, under each of the headings. For sure, you need to be comfortable with the headings, but also this is your first piece of scaffolding. Whichever model you choose will become the working model for the whole team. You need to be able to train them to always think around these headings when you ask them to look above the parapet of the daily grind and think long term, creatively and pragmatically.

Therefore we have a couple of provisos on the model you use: (1) does it encompass all of your accountabilities? And (2) does it stretch the mind sufficiently without getting silly? Too complicated and your team will gaze at you blankly, too simple and you miss out on valuable opportunities for insight.

There are some key reasons for establishing accountability:

- Other people will judge you by what you deliver, both successes and omissions, so best you all know up front.

- Some key areas, crucial to overall success, simply do not appear on weaker managers' radar, e.g. employee development. They think that is an activity only addressed by training courses – something that somebody else does.

- Gaps in accountability can be apparent after the event; something goes wrong and at the inquest no one person can get the blame. Rest assured, all those connected with the incident will get a share.

I saw a documentary on the television some time ago about a British ship on the eve of the Iraq war. They were preparing to take part in an American 'owned' exercise at sea before the war started, and at the debriefing the next morning the captain pointed out that someone should have made themselves accountable for obtaining the weather report. Without it, they had only discovered at the last moment that they could not take part in the exercise and there were red faces all round. He said, very calmly under the circumstances, that he expected all the officers on board to ensure that they knew what they were all accountable for so that nothing would slip through the net again.

Okay, so not many of us are about to do battle, but the point remains the same, as indeed the same red faces appear at management meetings all over the land.

Possible models

First, let me introduce you to McKinsey 7-S. Tom Peters and Robert Waterman's model is known as the McKinsey 7-S because they were consultants with McKinsey at the time. Originally published in an article 'Structure is Not Organization' (1980), there are seven elements to consider (Table 1.2). The hard Ss are usually easy to identify by looking in strategy documents and business plans. The soft Ss are difficult to nail down because they are about the way people work and systems set up for people management. The theory is that effective organisations achieve a fit

Table 1.2   McKinsey 7-S (Peters et al., 1980)

What are you accountable for?	
Hard Ss	
Strategy	Plans
Structure	How the company is organised – which bits of the structure are yours?
Systems	Procedures, processes and routines for anything
Soft Ss	
Style/culture	Dominant
Staff	Numbers and types of people
Skills	Capabilities
Shared values	Interconnecting centre of all the elements – beliefs and behaviours that guide actions

between all the elements and if one element changes it will affect the others.

Next, the Balanced Scorecard. This was popularised by Robert Kaplan and David Norton, initially in the USA, at a time when managers were recognising that too much emphasis was being put on purely financial measures in business. This particular model is primarily designed to get you to measure performance by setting objectives and designing measures to suit your unique situation, but in all areas not just financial:

- financial perspective
- internal process perspective
- customer perspective
- innovation and learning perspective.

Now, neither of these models was designed specifically to help you define your accountabilities so it will take some creativity to use the headings as a guide.

Skills tips

- Do a brain dump first, with the large glass in your hand should you wish.
- Don't just write the obvious, think outside the normal list.
- Write stretching accountabilities.
- You might not believe that you are expected to go above and beyond the call of duty, i.e. the apparent scope of your job, but the best managers do. They use their initiative to spot issues beyond the confines of their area, and they are the ones to suggest meetings to solve problems. They take the first step.

The way we do things round here (values)

You know, and I know, that every organisation has a different feel to it, a different way of doing things on a daily basis. As managers, we soon know if we can personally fit in with that particular way. For example, are you more comfortable in a steady, hierarchical structure with rules and protocols, or would you prefer to be into something more entrepreneurial with no rules?

However long you have been with an organisation it's worth trying to pin down 'the way we do things round here'. Try getting some words down on paper – properly constructed phrases that mean the same thing to anyone who reads them.

What does the team think?

This time start from the bottom up and ask your team first. Try one or more of these questions:

- How would you say we do things round here?
- What sort of behaviour is valued the most?
- What are the unwritten rules?
- What's the best way to get things done?
- What happens when things go wrong?

Do the values match the glossy posters?

Some organisations have these values written down on posters or handy pocket-sized cards. The thing is, do the glossy words match what actually goes on? To be fair, if the organisation has consulted with the sharp-end workers, the values are usually accurate. Even if the people at the top have simply imposed the values they could still be lived with. For example, a small independent school, part of a larger group but with its own unique identity, was taken over by a much larger concern. Their new values arrived by courier with instructions to pin on the wall so every parent and child could marvel and be impressed. The staff examined them minutely, as teachers do, and were satisfied that they could happily live with them; they were pretty laudable – couldn't argue with those.

But here is the crux of the matter – the Head said, 'we can't just make a decision at a meeting and say "Oh good, we can tick that value box." We have to look for ways to make them happen – and one or two of those values will take some thinking about'. That lucky parent organisation had a Head with sense as well as brains.

Another conversation I had with the chief executive officer of a 1,000-strong organisation went along these lines:

CEO: 'Flossie (another director) is keen to get our organisational values sorted out and written down.'

Me: 'Not a bad idea, then you can work out what mechanisms you have in place to make the values actually happen. It'll be a useful exercise – you might find some gaps but it'll be worth it in the long run'.

CEO: 'Mechanisms – like what?

Me: 'Oh ... your reward system, meeting structures, communication – messages etc.'

CEO: Silence and look of horror.

The point is, does the value system match the rhetoric? Back to Goldman Sachs again. Their values are (1) Client first, and (2) Teamwork. Professor Davidson pointed out that the idea of putting teamwork very high was interesting in the land of investment banking. 'Now most investment banks operate on the values of "you eat what you kill", in other words you are evaluated as an individual purely on the revenue you bring in'. At Goldman Sachs, however, the person who builds long-term client relationships, develops people and mentors them will get a higher bonus than someone who is arrogant and selfish but achieves higher revenue. This organisation has set its values and embedded the mechanisms to support them.

Positive action

Enough thinking on this, whatever the state of your particular nation, *you* have to work your way through the minefield, so get the answers to these lined up for your own department.

- How do the team and I describe the way the way things are done round here?

- Does this description fit with any values actually written down and promoted in the organisation?

- Does this fit with me? Can I work like this? (If the answer is no, look for another job.)
- If I am comfortable with these values, does my team actually act them out?
- If they don't why not?
- Have I got to re-educate them?
- Are there mechanisms in place to support the values, e.g. pay, promotion, communication methods?
- Can I look for and encourage actions in my area that will make the values happen?
- Are we doing anything contrary to the values?
- Can I offer some constructive suggestions higher up for the whole organisation?
- Even if nobody else is acting out these values what can I do in my area to make them work?

And finally:

- What are my own beliefs that will add to the values? What ways of working are important to me to see in my team?

For example:

> 'This team's going to be a learning team. We are going encourage ideas and responsibility, even risk-taking, and we are not going to dish blame when it goes a bit pear-shaped'.

or:

> 'We are going to have the best controlled costs, lowest wastage, and highest profit in the whole enterprise'.

'We are going to be the initiators round here – the ones that look beyond our boundaries for opportunities to improve'.

Whatever your values are, nail them down and act them out every day. Get the whole team thinking and acting on the same standards. You will get different ideas about how to skin the cat (100+) but that's all to the good. The rest of the chapters in this book will give practical tips on how to embed, that is what to 'do' about, your values.

At this point you just need to get your ducks in a row.

Create your own business plan

'What?!' I hear you say, that's for finance directors and entrepreneurs, not poor old middle managers. Well let me tell you it's a cathartic experience, and not for the faint hearted, but boy does it make life easier further down the line.

Buy a book on it if you like – preferably a simple one with lots of charts and questions – not too much text. Alternatively, use the following template to get you started. Remember you are not going to have to present this to your bank manager. This is a process that will get everybody's ducks in a row; yours', your teams' (the principal players in all of this exercise) and even your line manager's (because they might have been a bit vague up till now).

Besides, you have already done a lot of the groundwork – it won't require many more brain cells to get it all down on paper. And the most useful part of this exercise will be getting your team involved. Of course, doing it this way will take longer, and require more patience, but the alternative is to do all the work yourself and present a state of the nation address to the team. Just tell them how you want it. Well maybe that's tempting and, depending on their personalities, they might prefer that you just tell them. But it just will not be good enough in the long run. You will use up valuable stress levels and time later on when you have to re-explain, re-sell, remind and so on. So involve them now, trust me, you *will* get payback.

Background information required

No matter the level of team involvement you will need to gather all the evidence that is available:

- company vision and purpose
- company PESTLE
- company SWOT
- your own accountabilities
- company values
- your own values
- company business plan (headlines plus the detail that relates to your own area)
- company strategy.

The next step is to pull out the information you need for your area. There will be gaps but you can fill those later. For now we need the preset ideas, especially the non-negotiables. At the end of this exercise you might feel the need to revisit the non-negotiables and actually negotiate a few but we are getting ahead of ourselves here.

Remember this is not for the bank manager; this is for you and your team so that you all end up in the same clearly-defined direction. That direction may very well change at a later date but at least you all started off on the same foot.

And because it's not for the bank manager we can start off simply; profit and loss forecasts and cash flow forecasts can all come a lot later, if ever.

The ultimate aim is to have a micro-strategy for your area. It's a fact, the best managers do.

Methods

Scenario 1

Look at Figure 1.1. One manager I know gives this single piece of paper to his team leaders and they in turn ask each individual to contribute their ideas on how they can collectively achieve this. All ideas are welcome. The team leaders and the manager collate the ideas onto one side of A4 beneath the figures and the document is then discussed at the next team meeting.

However, this team already knows exactly where the business should be in the market and has also had the benefit of regular communications from on high, as regards current thinking on service and customers.

Scenario 2

Another group of managers, from a completely different business, had never sat down and collectively agreed where they were in the market place, nor indeed what level of service they should be offering. The goalposts had in fact moved over the last few years and although some managers knew exactly where they had moved to, others were still playing on a different pitch!

They had to start the business plan exercise from scratch before they consulted their teams. As a group they pulled together the initial plan on market position and offering. It

Figure 1.1 One-year business plan for department x

Organisation's main objectives for the year
1.
2.
3.
4.
5.
Estimated sales for the year
Estimated sales monthly
Any other headline figures that are important? e.g. wastage, customer acknowledgment rates, staff costs as a per cent of sales
What do you sell? ■ Products: Number of types, ranges ■ Services: Define the service
What is your market position? ■ High quality and price? ■ High volume, low price?
Who is your target audience? ■ Public/business to business/retail shops ■ Describe them e.g. top-end/SMES/etc
How do you reach your customers? ■ Marketing campaign: describe it ■ Sales rep ■ Passing trade
Who are your suppliers? ■ Describe them
How do you sell your products/services? ■ Direct to the customer? ■ Through an intermediary? ■ Describe your level of service?
After sales service ■ Delivery service? Which areas? ■ What after sales service do you offer?
Who are your competitors? ■ What do they offer that you do not?

was a tad painful for those managers who had previously been playing on a different pitch, but everyone was happy in the end (albeit some considerable time after for one or two) that they had a common set of goalposts.

Scenario 3

This organisation is set up to regularly create and review business plans using the McKinsey 7-S model. We look at this in more detail, along with other options, in Chapter 2; however, suffice to say at this point that you can make your business plan as sexy as you wish.

Business plan summary

The key to this concept of business plan creation is to keep grounded by being sure what you are using it for – the main aims of the exercise. And these are:

- *You* need a clear direction for the activities of your team over the next year.
- Your team needs clear direction and tramlines to work within.
- Everybody needs to be involved in the design to some extent, otherwise they just stay on the sidelines.
- The design needs to fit the business and the audience, i.e. the team. Too complicated and you lose them, too simple and the complex people think it is silly.

Remember though:

- All managers need to work to the same organisational objectives and market position. Major disagreement among your management group will need to be resolved at some stage soon. If there is an elephant problem in the room, best you all acknowledge that it's there and work out how to get rid of it. Elephants do grow, and managers soon find themselves preoccupied with feeding them rather than getting on with the job in hand.

- Business plans need to be written so that the team understands every word.

- It is not part of your accountability to design an agreed business plan for the whole organisation. You could proactively, albeit subtly, encourage the idea; indeed, you should if you are to be among the premier league of managers. However, the very least you should do is have one for your own team. Anything less will create extra work along the line.

Scaffolding summary

- As middle managers we have to clarify organisational direction and values so that our department has clear direction.

- People do not work well in a reactive environment – we can only do our best in a proactive atmosphere. And it is the responsibility of middle managers to shape that proactive atmosphere. The starting point to that is direction.

- A description of tasks for which we are responsible is not enough. We need to identify the full scope of our accountability. You can be sure that senior managers know what they think we should be doing.

- Involving the team in business planning is a powerful piece of scaffolding, for you and them, and has long-term benefits.

Beginning the scaffolding frame (information processes)

This is where the building work begins for you. I am sorry to be the bearer of bad news here, but the whole construction plan is solely down to you as the manager. Of course, your organisation may very well have some, or plenty, of processes in place. The thing is, do they work; do they help get the job done? Do they actually *help* you manage the whole shooting match or just cause irritation and extra work?

You cannot, of course, *do* the whole job from beginning to end yourself. So get ready to *manage* the whole thing. You need practical actions to sort out which processes you will or will not need.

We should have in mind here a set of routine actions to enable you to keep people on track, encourage usable ideas, and solve problems when they arise – because they certainly will. The processes need to be neat and simple, covering all the bases, giving you all the opportunities you need to keep a grip on activities, and finally leading to results.

We talk about organisations as if they are 'its', a kind of separate being, from which we the managers/workers are somehow divorced. Of course, it has been said many times before that this is not true; an organisation is the sum of its people, not a thing of its own. So there's nothing new in that, we all know that *we*, the people, are the organisation.

For the purpose of this exercise though, we *will* think of 'it' like a building, maybe a cathedral, maybe a Portakabin – you choose – the building itself is neither here nor there. And you, the workers, need to build a framework of scaffolding to work on this building.

The scaffolding has to be robust, used a lot, and accepted as the norm by all around you. The good news is that the processes can and will change. Just because the first set of scaffolding seemed like a good idea at the time does not mean you have to stick with it. Dismantle some if you need to, and put it back up again later if times change.

A key set of scaffolding, in my experience, has to be erected around communication and information flow, and another set around reward and recognition. The most used and abused though, appears in Chapter 4 – meetings. Always guaranteed to make managers raise their eyes heavenwards – just mention meetings, more meetings and the barriers go up. Well just to warn you, they are only a few chapters away.

In the meantime let's look at what we need to cover with these processes:

1. How you get the information you need to do the job for which you are accountable.

2. How you ensure information gets to your team.

3. How they get it back to you.

4. How you apply knowledge to that information.

5. How you handle the excesses of other people's behaviour.

In summary, this chapter is about how you channel what people know and how they behave when they know it. Too much information is a turn off, too little prevents efficiency, and extreme behaviour can ruin the whole enterprise.

Get your scaffolding assembled

Now is the time to think about the processes you will need and the most logical order to assemble them. As you might expect there is more than one way to do this but for the time being try this for size.

Step 1: Your department's micro-strategy

It should cascade logically from the organisational strategy, but if there isn't one, no matter, just write your own (advice to follow, so don't be daunted). The work you did on the business plan gives you the basis of your micro-strategy.

Step 2: Operational plans

Flowing on from the strategy you will need a simple timed plan, with any measurements you can muster, showing quite clearly what everyone is trying to achieve. Depending on the nature of your job, the operational plan might need to be more detailed.

Step 3: Information flow

Who needs to know what, when and how; a map or chart with notes detailing information flow. Just putting the map together once every few years helps you think it through and cover all the bases.

Step 4: Knowledge management

Getting a bit more sophisticated here but don't shut the book just yet. It's only about turning data into knowledge, and how that knowledge is used.

Step 5: Networking

Get some processes in place that ensure that you and your team connect with others outside your day-to-day area of work.

Step 6: Glue

Do all the processes knit together? Are you doing something that conflicts or jars? Are they all joined up?

Step 1: Micro-strategy

Design

It would help you here if your organisation has a nice clear vision, strategy, and objectives for the next 6–12 months. But it really doesn't matter if they don't, because this is the point where you write your own. If you have done your homework from Chapter 1 then you have a reasonable idea of where the whole organisation is going, who the target customers are and the level of service you are offering (from your mini-business plan). This just needs to be converted into your department micro-strategy, which, at its simplest level, is a set of objectives for the next six months.

Alternative organisations

Organisation A has two objectives (out of five) for the next three years:

- to grow sales by 6 per cent annually to 2007;
- to grow margin by 3 per cent annually to 2007.

The manager's task is to work out how they will achieve these in their area, in their particular circumstances.

Organisation A uses a pyramid model with specifics towards the top and broader visions at the bottom (Figure 2.1).

Organisation B has a vision, which translates into:

- four key objectives each around sales, profitability and teamwork; with

- four strategies, one each for:
  - sales and marketing
  - business processes
  - employees
  - communication.

Each of these strategies, which support the overall vision and objectives are represented as four strategy pillars, so the visual looks like Figure 2.2:

Organisation C uses the McKinsey 7-S and Organisation D the Balanced Scorecard (see Chapter 1).

Figure 2.1 Pyramid strategy model with specifics towards the top and broader visions at the bottom

Sales

Margin

Staffing Levels

Channels to market

High Performance

Figure 2.2 Four strategy pillars

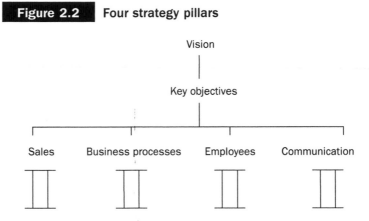

Vision

Key objectives

| Sales | Business processes | Employees | Communication |

These are only four examples of the same process. You may choose one of these, another known model, or design your own. The aim is to put together goals and a set of objectives for your team, under each of your chosen headings, which represent the steps you must all take to reach the organisation's goals and objectives.

Let's suppose in the absence of any sexy strategy document produced by senior management that you choose Organisation B's pillars for your model. In the light of the evidence you have gathered you should feel able to put together a simple strategy for your department using a template like Figure 2.3.

Just make sure that the objectives for your team are:

- in line with overall business objectives – it is pointless for you to go in a different direction from the organisation;
- SMART (see below);
- stretching but achievable – easy objectives do not grow profits;
- are 'bar room' readable, i.e. concise and clear for everybody;
- updated as targets are achieved.

Figure 2.3 Simple strategy template

By the end of Year 1 we will:			
Sales	Business processes	Employees	Communication

Optional but desirable actions

Involve the team in the design of objectives:

- get their ideas (see Chapter 4);
- especially get ideas from the main players – the part-timer who works eight hours a week may not have many but at least listen to them.

Add in performance measurements:

- SMART objectives should be robust enough but if you and/or your organisation actually measure success rates in certain areas then it is worth adding in the measures against the relevant objective, e.g. number of customer visits, error rates. We will consider the best way to do this next.

The technicalities not to be missed

SMART objectives

- *Specific*: A specified task and end result – precise outcomes; quantifiable or testable.
- *Measurable*: Quantitative or qualitative.
- *Attainable (agreed)*: Challenging but perfectly possible (and agreed – nobody will achieve an objective they don't agree with).

- *Realistic*: Achievable within defined constraints such as time, money etc.
- *Time bound*: Within a set period of time.

For example: To increase output by 10 per cent (specific) by the end of the quarter (timed) using a new machine and new shift working system (attainable and realistic).

Performance measurements

There are many books and a mass of advice on performance measurements so we can assume that designing them is not as easy as it might seem. The two most important things to remember in my view are:

- Not many people find them easy, so go for it and get the team to help you – together you will write better measures than the senior managers would on their own.
- Whatever you measure will be in the front of people's minds and will therefore influence their day-to-day actions. For example, just measuring the number of complaints will make people less likely to report them, and maybe also create a blame culture. It would be better to measure the number of complaints that have been settled to the customer's satisfaction. This is more likely to encourage positive behaviour when things go wrong, and still allows you to see what actually went wrong in the first place so you could look for patterns. This measure accepts that problems will occur, but you care much more about how they are dealt with.

If you do add in performance measures for the department they will only be useful if they are:

- clear and concise, and therefore easily understood by all;
- measuring a positive action, and therefore good for all, especially the customer;
- inexpensive to measure;
- directly related to people's actions, not the weather or interest rates, which are out of our control.

Take care to measure effectiveness as opposed to just data, e.g. for an admin department 'words per minute' represents data, whereas per cent of correct documents produced measures effectiveness.

Skills tips

Objectives

- Sometimes people get so focused on the objective they lose sight of the bigger picture, e.g. the stock controller whose main objective was to maintain a certain level of stock kicked up a huge fuss when all their stock in one area was sold to one customer to get them out of a difficult situation. Their need to meet the objective overrode the need to meet customer expectations. Just help people keep their perspective.
- Keep your eye on accountability and don't let objectives become the whole focus. Remember that we normally spend 90 per cent of our time on accountabilities and 10 per cent actually working on objectives.

Look off your own radar

- The purpose of the micro-strategy is to keep all activities channelled in the right direction but do not forget to look beyond your own radar on a regular basis. Make sure you have a pretty good idea of what's going on around you and in the outside world. This may ultimately affect what your team does. Another competitor or supplier becoming slicker might impact on you. A change in customer activity might be the tip of an iceberg. Another department's success or failure might cause you to re-evaluate your strategy. And so on ... Any one of the following sections may cause you to re-think and adjust.

Achievable time lines

- Be realistic about what can be achieved and by when.

Step 2: Operational plans

Can you imagine a buildings and facilities manager with a five-year spending plan and no other sort of plan whatsoever? They have a budget for day-to-day maintenance and big pockets of money for major building works. So the money is nicely allocated, but how about the work? In reality the entire team leads a fire-fighting existence in between major projects, stressful enough but when the big projects start it becomes excruciating. People go sick regularly and the main set of values are based on 'go as slow as possible' because nobody ever feels they are on top of anything, not ever.

What our buildings manager needs is a plan of works (operational plan) preferably to cover a) long-term preventative work and b) shorter-term maintenance. Jobs can then be allocated to people with end dates. That then means that time spent on urgent jobs is minimised and the fire-fighting decreases.

If your work is project-based then you will be used to working in this way, with plans and timelines, responsibilities and review dates. But a lot of us have some projects, alongside our main ongoing accountabilities, and now a few objectives.

Traffic light plans

A really helpful process to put in place for any type of work is an operational plan with a traffic light or red, amber, green (RAG) system. Don't include day-to-day work – that can stay on a works plan, if at all – but certainly put in all projects and department objectives.

Organisation A reviews its plan monthly, it includes:

■ department objectives

■ projects

■ marketing plan

■ specific activities with no objectives, e.g. performance reviews.

Each component has a target figure (per cent or date or numbers) and actual. The actual is colour coded at the review date

Red	=	behind plan
Green	=	above/exceeding plan
Amber	=	±5 per cent target

Organisation B puts together a more comprehensive plan at the beginning of each year, following the McKinsey 7-S, and including topics such as issues, risks, assumptions. Each department and many individuals have their own plans and all plans are publicly (internally) reviewed each quarter.

Organisation A is not so public. Each team leader is required to base their monthly report on the traffic light report with a summary of progress in bullet point format only, and comments only required for the 'red' markers.

This department used to review the plan round the table at the monthly meeting but it became huge, and team leaders switched off when not on 'their bit'. Now they have one meeting at the beginning of the year for each team leader to present, discuss and agree their objectives. From then on, the RAG rated monthly reports are circulated to each team leader and the department manager reviews each line quarterly with the relevant team leader.

Both organisations say that the RAG system puts real emphasis on objectives and performance, 'It makes objectives real, certainly clarifies expectations, and fits objectives into the bigger picture'.

Skills tips

In Organisation B the departments spend a night and a day, once a quarter with the whole team planning, reviewing and goal setting. They use the same mode each time so that every individual is 'coached' to think around the same structure, but also forced into thinking outside their own 'field'. They are also 'coached' to consider 'cause and effect'. One valid point to consider is that every single team member in this organisation is highly qualified and technical. In theory they have the brain cells to contribute effectively and intelligently. In practice their technical and academic expertise makes it imperative that they see the bigger picture, otherwise they may sink quietly into their own highly intelligent box.

Organisation A has quarterly management only meetings. Managers then go back and communicate with their less academic teams.

Whichever way you do it, make sure you are asking people for answers that you are fairly sure they have, even if they have to dig deep, especially the first time. And make sure you have avenues to include everyone; the coal-face people usually have appropriate answers to problems and sometimes inappropriate answers too, and they can often see the obvious, which may be eluding you.

How far you go with this

Nobody enjoys working for a reactive manager, it's certainly not exciting. The hamster wheel style of existence suits nobody, so let everyone get off for a while and get some achievable plans in place to action and review (trust me, you'll all feel better for it).

How you view the overall responsibility

The best managers see their role as running a series of projects: task-based, people-focused, systems-based, research work and so on.

Creativity

Organisation B likes to get its managers thinking creatively so they are asked to make some assumptions for five years' time. This is off most people's radars and can lead to some wild ideas, especially when they get to the end of the five years and see where they are, as opposed to where they thought they might be. The point is that it really gets managers looking above and beyond. The thinking is that if this becomes a regular exercise, the brain is trained to become more creative.

Step 3: Information flow

Designing information scaffolding could be a full-time job in itself. Who needs to know what, and which media to use, are questions even the experts struggle with. For us though, these are key processes to get in place. We need quality communication for the sake of efficiency and morale, and our own sanity. The circle in Figure 2.4 (Icke, 2003) shows the full extent of the scaffolding required but the eight stages are simple enough.

1. *What preparation or planning is needed?* (preparation and planning)

2. *What method or medium do you use to communicate?* (media)

3. *What message do you want to communicate?* (message)

| Figure 2.4 | The Eight-Stage Communication Circle (Icke, 2003) |

The 8-Stage Communication Circle

repeat, reinforce message	monitor/measure progress			Telephone	1-2-1
				Team meeting	Letter
publish actions	**Outcome & follow up**	**Media**		Presentation	Email
chase actions					
pre-reading	**Preparation & planning**		**Message**	3 main points	
rehearse				concise,	
distribute information				clear	
active listening	**2-way**	**Audience**		manager	supplier
feedback, surveys				subordinate	customer
	Situation/process	**Style**		fair process	formal
	monthly meeting			exploratory	informal
	appraisal			team briefing	chat

4. *Who needs to know?* (audience)

5. *What process or situation you use?* (process)

6. *What is your style?* (style)

7. *How do you check for understanding?* (two-way)

8. *What do you want to happen as a result of the communication?* (outcome/follow-up).

Reporting processes

With the eight-stage circle in mind, we need to identify the key scaffolding.

Reports to you

We have already talked about RAG rating reports. You need to think about how often you really need written reports, to what depth, and who from. Everything depends on the nature of your business and the timeframes you have to work to.

Remember there are several benefits to formal reports as opposed to verbal updates.

1. You receive information you can absorb at a time of your choosing, and have time to think of appropriate questions.

2. The writer has to stop, get their thoughts in discipline for the reporter; stopping and reflecting minimises emotional, reflex responses. Concise articulation conveys information clearly and simply, taking up less of the recipient's time.

3. You all have a record you can revisit after time to see patterns or significant turning points. This is useful, but not imperative if you have other mechanisms in place.

Benefits 1 and 2 are the most powerful.

Whichever type of report is appropriate for your business here are some general guidelines to follow:

- Keep to a standard template for everybody, using the same headings or questions.
- Always include department and individual objectives so that they are constantly in focus for you and the writer.
- Long reports, should have a single page summary of the headline points at the front.
- RAG ratings and bullet points are good.
- Circulate copies to the right people, not everyone who might be remotely interested.
- Create a discipline of 'on-time' reporting, in other words, create a fuss if one is late otherwise deadlines will slip downhill quickly.
- Show that you read them by reacting to the content using praise, questions, taking action etc.
- Invest time up-front in a short training session for all reporters and then give people instant feedback on style and presentation. Reporting information accurately and concisely is a skill we do not all possess, and usually not one considered entirely necessary to do a job well. It is, however, a skill everyone should try to acquire.

Reports to the team

We often do this verbally at meetings; heaven knows people cannot be trusted to read documents properly, if at all! There is a case though for an appropriate written report – the trick is to find what is appropriate for your people and business. Here are some options to consider:

1. Weekly bulletins containing what I would call the 'church notices': simple facts, changes to rules, reminders, e.g. for

'no throwing confetti outside the church', substitute 'smokers are reminded to use the bus shelter in the yard, smoking elsewhere may lead to disciplinary action'. These bulletins are good to circulate and have everyone sign.

2. Monthly newsletters in addition to, or in place of non-existent, organisational newsletters. You could design your own and delegate responsibility to team members on a rota basis. Certainly keep it punchy, perhaps with bullet point links to where people can find full documents or expert knowledge. The team could find other contributors and publish letters of thanks. Getting rotating individuals to take charge promotes different styles and creativity as well as ownership. It may be seen as a chore but if it's getting over good quality information it's worth it.

3. Turn over the main notice board to a living report. Most people walk straight past notice boards, but if you could somehow create an ever changing board space with pizzazz and everyone's involvement, it could become a focal point.

Two-way mechanisms

1. Originally, I believe, a Sears' idea, some organisations have white boards where staff can write their ideas/gripes/questions and the relevant manager must write the answer.

2. One organisation I know invites anonymous letters to the in-house magazine with answers printed from the relevant director. Letters are guaranteed to be published, and answered, unless they are libellous. Needless to say these are the first pages that readers turn to.

   The directors say that this is rather like managing in a goldfish bowl. They are accountable for everything in their area, quite literally. One director said it was good for him; if he had a decision to make he just had to anticipate the anonymous letter and his response. If he could justify the decision coherently in print he would be ok.

Skills tips

I once had someone working for me who was extremely efficient, dotted every 'i' and crossed every 't', but the trouble was the efficiency went too far. He did not want the department caught out in anyway, so he developed systems to back up the primary routines. Logs recording papers in and out were a great favourite as I recall.

'So how many times did we get chased last year by x department for those papers?' I asked.

'Oh, twice and it took 30 seconds each time to tell them the date the papers went out'

'How long would it have taken you to have checked the work was done and papers sent *without* the log?'

'Well I knew they would have gone, we always send the papers on, but checking the folders would have taken maybe 10/15 minutes'

'And how long do you spend on the log each year?'

'Heavens knows ...'.

So we abandoned the log and kept up the pressure on everyone to process papers efficiently with a 24-hour turnaround. Fred lost some peace of mind but gained many hours in time.

Step 4: Knowledge management

If you search the Web you will be able to access some superbly intelligent articles and books on the subject of knowledge management, but for now it is worth our while dwelling on the topic in sufficient depth only to help you implement processes that encourage greater *knowledge* sharing, as opposed to pure *information*.

There is always talk of *information* access and sharing (IT being the prime mover here) but *knowledge* crops up far less as a word in common usage in our daily work. First let's start with a definition of information and knowledge from the Association for Information Management (ASLIB):

> *Information*: An assembly of data in a comprehensive form capable of communication and use.
> *Knowledge*: Information evaluated and organised in the human mind so that it can be used purposefully.

So, most organisations spend time on *information* management, but good managers should spend time on *knowledge* management because knowledge is valuable. Unfortunately it is difficult to grab hold of, mainly because it is in peoples' minds, not on a hard disk somewhere.

What is information and knowledge management?

According to Macdonald:

> *Knowledge Management* is the process of making creative, effective and efficient use of all the knowledge

and information available to an organisation for the benefit of its customers and thus the company.

Knowledge is therefore an intellectual asset which in the new global economy will become more important than traditional capital assets. (Macdonald, 1999)

Importance of good information management

Figure 2.5 shows the DIKAR model (Venkataram, 1996). The model starts with basic data, which is interpreted by people into information, added to knowledge, which in turn brings about informed actions, which in turn generate business results.

So now we know straight away that information management (IM) covers data, information and knowledge. We also know that good IM is important because it directly affects our actions, and therefore results, in business.

The model is useful because it shows what IM is, why it is important and the levels of information that we work with in business today.

Many experts also suggest that starting to think about what you want to achieve with data and information (results) rather than looking at data in isolation first, is a better approach to take.

Figure 2.5   The DIKAR model (Venkataram, 1996)

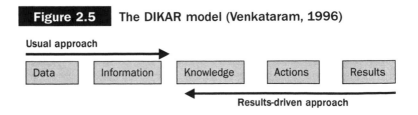

Actions to take

Your main aim is to train your team to interpret information, forecast and share knowledge. To do this you will need to use your meeting structure wisely by allocating time to this. However the good news is that it's not something to be done separately but should be done in conjunction with other activities.

So every time you get together to design the micro-strategy, agree objectives, share information, however often that may be, apply the same model of thinking to the talking.

Lucey's approach (1997) to planning and decision making encourages us to work backwards from the 'results section' in the DIKAR model:

- *What are we trying to achieve here?* What quantifiable end result do we want? (strategic)

- *What actions do we need to take to get there?* What are the required supporting actions, e.g. a change in resources, systems? (tactical)

- *What immediate resources do we need?* (operational)

- *What's got to happen now?* (current operational)

Skills tips

- Always broaden the team's horizons by pushing the strategic results driven approach. Ask them to quantify or describe the results that could be achieved in five years' time, even if they prove to be way off beam, they will have lifted their heads above the parapet, got outside the usual box.

- When we start to think like this, we start talking 'the knowledge'; maybe sometimes it's only opinion, but if you dig to find out what the opinion is based on, you will come across the knowledge, and because it has been said, it becomes shared.

- Any reporting to the team on information should be interpreted in order to gather the knowledge. Don't let people just say 'well, this has happened and this is how we dealt with it'. Ask for the lessons learned for the next time, which inevitably exposes the knowledge.

- For decisions you make repeatedly, consider the impact elsewhere as a sort of routine. If everyone must think it through and speak up, more knowledge becomes available.

Step 5: Networking

The best middle managers are good 360-degree networkers. This simply means that they connect with people across the business. To start with they keep contacts going in a range of fields: finance, HR, marketing, to name a few. Then there are regular chats with other managers beyond the task in hand, after the meeting, before the meeting, in the corridor, over a sandwich, whatever.

It is difficult to do this if you are not naturally easy with other people, or indeed if time pressures are bearing down on you. However, it is worth developing business conversations even if you find it hard to just chat.

What you are aiming for is a personal radar for picking up issues outside your own immediate field. From there you will be able to propose solutions or initiate meetings. This proactive style stands you out from the crowd and commands respect all round.

It doesn't mean that you bowl in telling other people how to run their areas, just that you are the one who spots the issues and initiates problem-solving.

Another level to consider for your network is externally: pick and choose carefully because there may well be too many external events you could attend locally. It is most useful to pick a) events that update your professional development, and not necessarily in your immediate field, and b) networks of interesting people who could be useful contacts now and in the future.

Skills tips

- Good people in apparently supporting roles (like the MD's secretary) can be just as important as the HR or finance manager. High-level information, when it's on offer, is useful in one way as is sharp end day-to-day information. Big picture and forward thinking give you a better perspective for your day-to-day decisions. Nitty-gritty problem areas, however, are often known by the sharp-end workers and ignored by most others.

- Try mapping out in rough who you should be networking with and then draw lines to the ones that you do actually see often. A visual map helps you to see the missing links more clearly (Figure 2.6).

Then work out how you might start to develop the other contacts, perhaps by going to check on something yourself, asking a question and then follow on with a more general chat.

- Many middle managers or senior managers in years gone by have found it extremely useful to have a mentor; mentors are not a trendy innovation. Having someone more senior, far more experienced, in a similar field, that you respect, to give advice and steer you can be extremely powerful both in terms of how you perform and your

Figure 2.6 Visually mapping network links

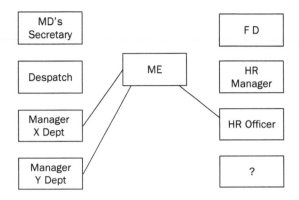

future career. You must respect them and they must respect you and both of you must be prepared to devote the time necessary. Mentors cannot be allocated; you must choose one.

Step 6: Glue

There is a tendency in many organisations for various people to introduce processes and initiatives to meet a particular need or whim. Maybe all these processes can be justified but when you stand back to look at the whole, it may be that they do not support the principal vision and aims of the business, they may conflict or overlap with each other.

At this point in the erection of the scaffolding you should just pulse check your own 'glue' situation by assessing your department on progress in the areas detailed in Panel 2.1.

Do not be too concerned if your grades are lower in the Glue section; we are heading on to those chapters now.

Panel 2.1: Is my scaffolding joined up?

Scoring

2 = The whole team understands and contributes to this process; other departments understand what we are aiming for

1 = A bit hit and miss – there is more work to do in this area

0 = Nowhere near it – I have to start planning how to achieve this

	Micro-strategy	Score
1	We have clearly defined objectives covering the key areas of our business, e.g. people, sales, profit, and information	
2	These objectives are reviewed regularly by the team	
3	It is clear to all of us how the department strategy connects with the overall business strategy	
4	The department strategy is 'bar room readable'	
5	Objectives are all SMART	
	Operational plans	
6	We have an achievable, stretching but realistic, plan suitable for our type of business	
7	Team members report to me on progress with the plan on a regular basis	
	Information flow	
8	All messages go out from me to using the appropriate media	
9	My team tells me everything I need to know without being asked all the time	

Panel 2.1: Is my scaffolding joined up? (*cont'd*)

	Information flow	Score
10	I translate corporate messages so that my team understands them	
11	We have good two-way communication in my team	
12	I communicate upwards effectively	
13	We keep systems simple and effective	
	Knowledge management	
14	As a team, we look at the results we want to achieve and then work out what knowledge we need to achieve those results	
15	We share knowledge effectively	
	Networking	
16	I connect with key people in the business on a regular basis	
17	I attend external networking events occasionally	
	Glue	
18	Every individual in my team knows exactly what is expected of them	
19	Every individual in my team receives the appropriate training to achieve all of the steps in this chapter	
20	I give praise when it is due	
21	I give constructive feedback to the team and individuals	

Panel 2.1: Is my scaffolding joined up? (*cont'd*)

	Glue	Score
22	I provide resources and support for people to do their jobs effectively	
23	I set performance standards which will enable us all to achieve our objectives	
24	People in my team are paid the right salary to fit with market rate and their effort	
25	We have the right amount of meetings to do our jobs well	
26	I can reward individuals who make extra special efforts	
27	People who under-perform are helped to achieve an acceptable performance	
28	I recommend people for other positions to enable them to develop their careers	
29	My team members connect with the right people outside our department on a regular and effective basis	
30	I feedback to senior managers constructive reports on progress and big picture issues	

The scaffolders
(off on the right foot)

Good managers invest time up front in getting people off on the right foot, not just after recruitment but also on a regular basis throughout their employment. The organisations where people like to work, and therefore work well, always employ some sort of mechanism which enables manager and managed to have a quality conversation at least once a year about the overall job role.

You might be tempted to tell me that your organisation includes this discussion at performance review time; there is perhaps a section on your form after all. Well, despite being on the form, some managers still forget to cover the issue and go leaping into the performance review and miss out step 1 which is actually a review of the job role and not the person.

To make the point clear, just imagine the worst case scenario, which we see a lot in our travels, where the employee has been appointed to a particular job and 10 or 20 years later everybody (except the employee) realises that they have made the job their own. The organisation needs to leap forward and dear old Flossie actually went in a totally different direction about eight years ago. We need the job role to reflect the needs of the business, not the person. So think roles here, not personalities.

We regularly come across such situations and always at the point where managers are pulling their hair out. Other people have moved on instinctively (even these managers have not had regular discussions with everyone about their job roles, so individuals have had to rely on common sense) and these sensible people are clashing against the old timers and fur is flying.

Quality conversations about job roles and accountabilities are a significant but simple process, not just because it makes sense to keep people moving with the times, but because they are far less threatening and uncomfortable than discussions about actual performance. By starting the conversation with the role, not the personality, hurt feelings are minimised. However, these conversations do not rule out what that person may bring to the job role in the future.

Quality conversation is the key here; no need for fancy systems. All you need to do is bring out the job description and talk it through once a year. Of course, if you have rubbish job descriptions, whatever document you use, it will take longer and be less constructive. You might, at the other extreme, have the sort of competency framework that is so agile it defrosts chickens as well. Lucky you.

The process is simple: a quality conversation about the job role, goals, expectations, and all that jazz, followed by a clear, concise summary of what you have both agreed on paper. Review it in six months or a year.

Skills tip

'Then you should say what you mean', the March Hare went on. 'I do', Alice hastily replied; 'at least – at least I mean what I say – that's the same thing, you know' (Lewis Carroll, 1866). Think about this in the bath tonight.

In this chapter we will look at the processes required to get people off on the right foot, even if they have been with you for the last 10 years.

- Step 1: Agree job role and accountabilities – you have accountabilities and so, therefore, should they.

- Step 2: Agree performance objectives, agree levels of initiative – how far do you want them to take their accountability?

- Step 3: Setting performance standards.

- Step 4: Providing resources to do the job.

- Step 5: Recruitment processes – a simple guide to appointing people who are a good fit with your team and values.

Step 1: Job role and accountabilities

Let me introduce you to Figure 3.1 – *The Performance Management Cycle* (Drucker, 1958).

Figure 3.1 The Performance Management Cycle (Drucker, 1958)

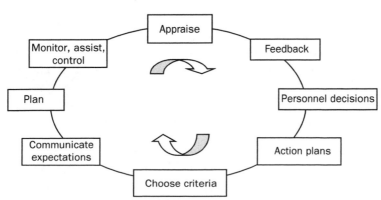

Reprinted from *The Practice of Management*, Drucker, P. Copyright 1958, with permission from Elsevier.

Where is the beginning of the cycle?

Choosing the criteria required for a particular job role and then communicating those expectations to the jobholder seems to be the only place to start. That said, a fair number of mediocre managers seem to think that employees have crystal balls, and so miss out the first stage altogether.

From Drucker's time, and ever since, good organisations have tried to clarify organisational, followed by individual, objectives and then support people in achieving the objectives. The cycle is completed with a robust and fair way of appraising performance. This is considered to be a comprehensive system of management; managers are forced to give emphasis to designing clear objectives for individuals and a formal plan for employee development before actually reviewing performance.

Basic steps of the objective-setting process

1. Agree principal accountabilities and main tasks.

2. Define objectives.

3. Define performance standards.

Armstrong (1994) suggests that managers and individuals can get together and agree work objectives by answering the following questions:

- What is the overall purpose of this job?
- What are the principal accountabilities or main tasks that have to be carried out to achieve that overall purpose?

- What corporate/functional/departmental objectives and values do we need to take into account in setting objectives for this job?

- In what specific respects can this job contribute to the achievements of those objectives and upholding corporate values?

- Taking each principal accountability or main task in turn, what, precisely, is the jobholder expected to achieve, expressed in the form of a target, a standard of performance, or a project or special task to be completed as appropriate?

- How will the manager and the jobholder know the extent to which objectives have been achieved (i.e. what are the performance measures or indicators)?

Headings for accountability

It would make sense to keep on using the same model throughout; as we have said before, that way everyone gets used to thinking along the same lines. It will just take a little athletic thinking to translate the model headings for your people. Try taking the McKinsey 7-S model, as it would appear the most tricky to translate, and apply it to an individual in your department (e.g. as might be shown in Fig 3.2).

Levels of initiative

We can spend good quality time on agreeing fine objectives with our team, but at the end of the day, people still need to know exactly how far they can go. That is the level of initiative you are expecting them to use in their everyday work.

| Figure 3.2 | Applying the McKinsey 7-S model to an individual in your department |

7-S Headings	What Flossie is accountable for:
Strategy	
Structure	
Systems	
Style	
Staff	
Skills	
Shared Values	

When I was first promoted to a more senior level of management, my MD at the time said, 'I have given you this job because I believe you are more than capable. Please do what you think is right for the business; you don't have to ask me every time. If however you have a question and my door is open, just bowl in. We will meet every fortnight and you can brief me on what you are up to or save up ideas that you want to discuss'.

Oncken and Wass (1974) identified five degrees of initiative that a manager can exercise in relation to the boss and to the system:

1. *Wait* until told (lowest initiative).

2. *Ask* what to do.

3. *Recommend*, then take resulting action.

4. *Act*, but advise at once.

5. *Act* on own, then routinely report (highest initiative).

They were thinking in terms of management initiative but I believe the principle applies to everybody. All staff need to be told at the outset which level of initiative you are expecting from them.

We really do not want people to be working to levels 1 and 2 unless they are new and inexperienced, but it is up to you to make it clear which of the other three levels you are generally looking for, and certainly allocate a level to specific tasks or projects as they are delegated.

Step 2: Agreeing objectives

Objectives may be:

- *Work objectives*: results to be achieved or the contribution required to achieve team or organisational goals.

- *Developmental objectives*: these concern individuals' goals to improve their performance, knowledge, skills and competence and will be covered in Chapter 6.

Work objectives can be defined at number of different levels:

- *Corporate*: organisation's mission, core values, etc (Chapter 1).

- *Departmental, then functional and team* (Chapter 2).

- *Down to individual*: job-related and should refer to the key result areas and key tasks that make up the individual's job (this chapter).

They can be set top-down and bottom-up. Top-down is ok but not guaranteed to be successful, even if you command respect and are an excellent salesperson. Bottom-up objectives can sometimes be amazingly stretching, but usually not what you had in mind at all. It would seem that the most successful route is, as usual, the joint approach.

The key to obtaining a whole set of individual objectives, which are agreed, stretching but achievable, and finally actually stand a chance of being carried out successfully, is joint discussion. You may need to suggest some, or all, but still involve individuals in their design.

Objective setting process

Agree team objectives first. If the team's objectives integrate well with the organisations', the team can be active in a bottom-up process. You can use the team's objectives to reinforce teamwork or any other value that is relevant to your organisation (remember the Goldman Sachs example.).

SMART objectives

We dealt with the structure of SMART objectives in Chapter 2, but here is another dimension to consider. A good performance objective will contain information about:

- *Performance*: what the task is and what the expected outcomes or behaviours are.
- *Condition*: the circumstances in which the task needs to be carried out, i.e. time, resource and cost constraints.
- *Standard*: the standards to which the task is carried out and the quality of the end result.

Here are the objectives for an assistant librarian in higher education for the next six months.

- To keep costs of the repair of undergraduate text books for the period January–June within budget by producing criteria for identifying which books should be repaired or rebound.
- To calculate the number of books ordered and measure the number of orders satisfied within the period January–June.

- To identify which data relating to final students are required from the Tutorial Department by the Library in the period January–June and to set up a two-way communication process to acquire this data.

- To come up with a plan for measuring how often routine tasks need to be carried out and a system for checking that they have been carried out.

- To implement a reporting system to ensure that in the absence of the head of department telephone messages regarding staff absences are noted and passed on to the head of department.

These objectives are unique to the first six months of that year, perhaps never to be repeated again unless the librarian falls at a particular hurdle.

Performance measures

We have already looked at performance measures for the department's micro-strategy in Chapter 2. In my view there are distinct advantages and disadvantages in trying to design measures for individuals.

Advantages

- People know, from the start, precisely which aspects of their performance are important and how they will be measured.

- The measurements will signify to everyone current priorities (but you can achieve a similar outcome with the department measurements).

- Individuals who are struggling can be given clear direction on exactly what they should be achieving.

- You could, if your organisation's pay scheme was set up this way, pay people according to their success in achieving their measurements. Plenty of organisations reward according to objectives achieved, just make sure they *are* achievable.

Disadvantages

- Sets of measures, unique to each individual, take a long time to write and are extremely difficult to get right.

- If you already have some sort of job description with the individual's clearly stated accountabilities, responsibilities and objectives why do you need extra measurements as well?

- Finding measurements for everything an individual does and knows is impossible. You end up measuring only the things you can, which results in assessing only part of a person's performance when actually you want to look at performance in the round, taking all skills into account.

In summary, the choice is yours. Agree measurements with individuals if you feel the need or your organisation rewards according to success in specific areas. But the measurements must be agreed and appropriate (as outlined in Chapter 2).

Do not spend years or even hours on this; let HR come up with a sensible framework of measures for the whole company. Give your input willingly though. I know one organisation that has taken three years to design an all-singing, all-dancing competency framework. Good for them, they will have an all-encompassing document to recruit, train and reward to, but in waiting for the framework, managers held their fire. The result was that a lot of managers worked without job descriptions or quality discussions with their people. Not constructive.

My advice is to get the job roles, accountabilities and overall department objectives nailed down and only move on to individual measurements if you feel the need.

The only exception to this would be if you have an individual who is struggling. Then it is an excellent idea to get a list of accountabilities down one side of a page with corresponding measurements down the right hand side. Getting measurements absolutely clear may very well avoid disciplinary action later on.

Writing measures

When it comes to individuals, think of their whole job role in terms of knowledge, skills and attitude. This helps give a holistic view, rather than focusing purely on actions, and therefore prompts you to think perhaps of areas you had not considered before. Combine this with the other headings for measurements discussed in Chapter 2: efficiency, effectiveness, adaptability. It might seem daft to write a performance measure for 'knowledge' – but perhaps the reason why the individual is not performing well is that they do not have all the knowledge necessary. For example, an HR officer not aware of ACAS guidelines or a salesman not aware of margins.

'Skills' performance measures are easier to define, but are often combined with attitudes.

Step 3: Setting performance standards

Steps 3 and 4 are small but significant. For a start, you set the standards, nobody else. Even though some come from health and safety, employment legislation or through company rules, it has to be you that leads the way and sets the tone.

Start off with a list of standards that are imposed from elsewhere and then add your own particular ones, e.g. a can-do attitude, make time to train others.

You already have some of the scaffolding in place to help you set and drive standards. In all the discussions you have with your team about strategy through to individual objectives, you have opportunities to set and reiterate standards. More scaffolding yet to appear in future chapters will also provide opportunities.

It is not something to be done once and revisited a year later; it is an ongoing bit of scaffolding, but you can, and should, engage your team leaders in the game. They all need to live and breathe the same standards.

Step 4: Providing resources

It is almost impossible to say precisely which processes you should put in place here, except to make some general, but significant points.

The first point is overarching them all – its up to you to get, argue for, and juggle resources.

If there can be a process to this it would have to be:

- Process: Your micro-strategy

  Action: Include an estimate of resources and communicate upwards

    Put together a cost benefit argument for more if necessary

    Allow for contingencies

- Process: Meetings (Chapter 4)

  Action: Review resources in operational plans on a regular basis

Step 5: Recruitment processes

If we believe that the four previous steps are important in getting people off on the right foot then, as managers, it is crucial that we get the right people to start with. The next time you have an opportunity to recruit for a role it would be wise to think though the 'what and the how' before embarking on what will most definitely be a costly and time-consuming exercise.

Yet again there are all sorts of books and websites offering detailed advice but let us just cut to the chase and keep it simple.

Bad managers just fill the vacancy with much the same as has gone before. Mediocre managers fill a vacancy with some sort of systematic process, usually laid down by the HR department. Excellent managers have:

- a bigger picture, manpower plan, even if it's just in their head;
- a robust selection process with several layers (one incisive interview isn't enough).

The bigger picture plan

Excellent managers have in their minds, and regularly revisit, the following points:

- The purpose of each job role defined and mapped in with all job roles in the department and connecting departments. (Don't think personality, think purpose of the job and how it fits/overlaps/or misses other roles).
- How much time it takes to do the job (not how long the last person took).

- Desired accountabilities mapped against the job purpose (e.g. the role purpose might be just to sell as much as possible, but the role holders might be accountable for high-level teamwork or problem-solving as well).

- A clear idea of how each person adds particular value to the defined job role (the extra they bring that might redefine the job or mean that you could manage with two good rather than three average people).

- Current and anticipated financial situation (your micro-staff costs vs. sales, the organisation's financial health and the state of the market).

- Company vision and strategy (types of products offered and plans for the future).

- Change (anything different on the horizon).

- State of the job market and your organisation's entry level into it (I knew a company years ago that recruited only from Oxbridge into its IT department, giving them a cheap entry-level and a massive collection of brain cells. The trouble was that after some great development in the role they all left to go to plum jobs in the city).

So the truly great managers have a good understanding of this picture and a micro-strategy in their heads for how they plan to fill future vacancies, if at all. They know which chess pieces need moving and when.

They also make robust financial cases to the powers that be for any proposed recruitment activity. 'It's going to cost this much, which I don't/do have in my budget, but the benefits will be X, Y and Z'. Preferably with some hard £ signs put on the benefits.

Understanding the job role

So you have the opportunity to recruit and if you have covered all the points in these first three chapters the next step should be easy. All the same, good managers revisit the job role just to get the clearest picture possible.

- Define job role, accountabilities, and level of initiative required:
    - listen to other people in the department and outside.
    - make sure it fits with your micro-strategy and the organisation's overall strategy.

Torrington and Hall (1991) suggest we gather information about the job:

- relationship with others
- all tasks and duties
- working conditions
- performance standards and objectives
- human requirements; the physical and psychological characteristics needed.

The job description

Not a list of tasks and duties – shame on you if yours are like this. However, we could at this point lose the plot and become obsessed with nailing down every task and behaviour. Indeed, a good HR manager will have already bullied all of you into writing some sexy job descriptions. But let's just keep it simple here. You need:

- job title
- reporting to (line manager)

- responsible for (team)
- job purpose
- key tasks (key result areas)
- key competencies (behaviours)
- current objectives/priorities
- limitations.

You might want to put the key result areas down one side and the competencies down the other.

A competency is generally defined as a behaviour and a competence as a minimum standard and is demonstrated by performance outputs.

Competencies have become more widely used, although not always in fancy frameworks, across the whole organisation. They are useful because they make us try to describe what we want in terms of behaviour rather than just the duties of a job. They might, for example, cover:

- team working
- communication skills
- people management/relationships
- customer focus
- results orientation
- problem solving
- planning and organising.

In the case of recruitment, competencies help us set objective criteria for all candidates and pre-set questions to gather information about the behaviours and outputs we are looking for. These competencies can then be used again for development and performance management, so they are the right sort of scaffolding in that they are ongoing and join up with other processes.

Some examples of communication competencies:

- takes time to listen to others;
- gives constructive feedback to colleagues;
- cooperates with others;
- effectively uses written communication.

Examples of results competencies:

- displays creativity in tackling problems;
- finds solutions that add value to customers and the business;
- builds long-term relationships with customers;
- shows commitment to delivering results;
- is able to adapt approach in order to obtain results.
  (from MSA Interactive 360 feedback tool)

Develop selection criteria

To increase objectivity and efficiency when sifting CVs and interviewing a simple approach is to identify selection criteria from the job description, rate them as essential or desirable, and then add a weighting score (e.g. see Figure 3.3). Reject candidates who do not meet the essential criteria and mark the rest.

Selection methods

According to Smith and Robertson (1986) interviews are only marginally better than astrology and graphology as predictors of ability to do the job. Higher up the prediction scale come personality tests, assessment centres, ability tests and work sample tests.

Figure 3.3 Shortlisting matrix with weighting

		Meets criteria	
Selection criterion	Weighting	Yes	No
Written communication			
Report writing	0.5		
Accurate form filling	2		
Understanding written instructions	2		
Letter writing	2		

Torrington and Hall (1991) suggest that it is unusual for one selection method to be used alone. A combination should be used dependent on a number of factors:

1. *Selection criteria appropriate for the post*: Group selection methods are useful for managerial posts.

2. *Acceptability and appropriateness*: Intelligence test may be insulting for CEOs.

3. *Abilities of the staff in the selection process*: Are they qualified?

4. *Administrative ease*: Individual interviews vs. a panel for only two candidates.

5. *Time factors*: Individual interviews rather than waiting for a group interview.

6. *Accuracy*: The more methods you use, the better the accuracy.

7. *Costs*: Tests cost a lot to set up but are cheaper to run thereafter, assessment centres cost a lot to set up and run, interviews are cheaper. Balance against the accuracy though.

The best organisations I know use a raft of methods and a pragmatic approach depending on the level of candidate. For example, Company A uses:

- An off-the-shelf personality test for all to provide the basis for further questions.
- Initial interview by HR and short-list interview by line manager.
- Key employees to provide a tour and answer questions, who are then consulted on their views on the short-list candidate.

Company B uses a full-blown assessment centre with a battery of tests and interviews.

Interview strategies

- *Frank and friendly (Hackett 1978)*

  Aim and advantage: Establishes rapport.

      People are more forthcoming.

      You create a favourable impression of company.

- *Problem solving (situational interview)*

  Aim and advantage: A hypothetical problem is set to evaluate competencies derived from the job description, only useful to test elementary knowledge, e.g. wires, drug dosages.

  Disadvantage: It is not good for predicting understanding and ability.

- *Behavioural event strategy*

  Aim and advantage: The difference from the problem-solving strategy above is that questions are asked about real situations the candidate has been involved in. This is more reliable, because you can ask what they predicted, what they did and why, and what they learned.

- *Stress strategy*

  Aim and advantage: The only time when you might use this strategy in an interview is using a time of war to select for espionage work (very aggressive style).

  Disadvantages: Stress strategies are attractive to some managers for the wrong reasons.

  Interviews are stressful enough and the style may be damaging to brand/image of company.

- *Sweet and sour strategy (Hackett 1978)*

  Aim and advantage: Here we have two interviews – (1) hard, (2) frank and friendly. The idea being that you get more in (2) after (1).

- *Sequential interviews*

  Aim and advantage: A series of individual interviews with appropriate parties. All must meet beforehand to agree assessment criteria and the efficiency of the operation. They give the employer a broader view of the candidate and allow the applicant a better view of many of the key people they will work with. It also requires considerable commitment from the candidate who may have to keep on repeating themselves.

■ *Interviews in tandem*

Aim and advantage: Only one interview but evaluation from two interviewers. Less formidable than a panel interview but still more difficult to develop rapport than with only one interviewer.

■ *Panel interviews*

Advantages: Share judgment.

A quick decision.

Less influenced by personal bias.

Ensures that the candidate is more acceptable to the organisation.

Allows the candidate to get a better feel for the organisation.

Disadvantages: Tribunal nature – sitting in judgment not having a conversation.

Little prospect of building rapport.

Just as much interplay between the panel members as between the panel and candidate.

One panel member can spoil another's line of questioning.

Interview structure

Interviews should have a beginning, a middle and a conclusion. It is a two-way process in which both parties have aims.

The interviewer's aims are to:

- further assess the candidate's suitability for the job role;
- paint a clear picture of the role and organisation;
- check that the candidate's information is valid;
- project an image of the organisation as a good employer.

The candidate's aims are to:

- find out enough to decide if they are suited to the job;
- clarify terms and conditions;
- find out how and when they will hear the results of their application.

There are a number of reasons why an interview should be structured according to Torrington and Hall (1991):

- The candidate expects the proceedings to be decided and controlled by the interviewer and will anticipate a structure within which to operate.
- It helps the interviewer to make sure that they cover all relevant areas and avoid irrelevant ones.
- It looks professional. Structure can be used to guide the interview and make it make sense.
- It ensures that the time available is used most effectively.
- It can be used as a memory aid when making notes directly after the interview.
- It makes it possible to compare candidates fairly.
- It helps to prevent discrimination and stereotypical assumptions.

Torrington and Hall's (1991) recommended structure is detailed in Table 3.1.

Table 3.1	Interview structure: a recommended pattern (Torrington and Hall, 1991)

Interview stage	Objectives	Activities
Beginning	Put at ease Develop rapport and set the scene	Greet by name, introduce self, neutral chat Agree interview purpose Outline how purpose will be achieved
Middle	Collect and give information, maintain rapport	Ask questions within the structure Structure might be biographical or based on areas of information or based on competences Listen, ask and answer questions
End	Close the interview and confirm future action	Summarise, check for more questions, say what happens next and when

Skills tips

1. Some questions to ask:
   - *What do you find is the best way to get things done?* (Are they results or procedure oriented? Bolshy or cooperative?)
   - *What has been your biggest challenge and how did you overcome the difficulties?* (Do they cave in easily? What represents a challenge to them and why?)
   - *What have been your greatest achievements at work?* (Quantifiable contributions)
   - *How would you describe the values of your last organisation and do they fit with your own?* (Will their values fit with yours?)

2. Don't go it alone; involve key players. It takes more time and arguments but in the long run everybody has a chance of win-win.

3. Gut feelings are OK (if in doubt, throw out) but don't rely on them. Try to get more scientific.

4. Don't wing it or talk too much.

5. Avoid stereotyping, and certainly do not discriminate.

Induction

Just a few words on induction. Getting new people up to speed as quickly as possible is in everyone's best interest and it is oh so easy to do. Keep it simple with:

■ a planned and timed programme;

■ a checklist of knowledge and skills to acquire;

■ appoint a buddy;

■ delegate monitoring the learning to the buddy;

■ arrange appointments with key players;

■ you could review progress at:

end of day 1 – informally

end of week 1 – informally

end of month 1 – formally

end of month 3 – formally

Scaffolding summary

■ Getting people off on the right foot at its simplest level requires only good quality discussion and agreement on the scope of the role, initiative, objectives and standards.

- If you are leading that discussion you will have to put words down on paper first, otherwise how will you know that people understand you properly?

- Some organisations use performance measures but this may be a step too far for some managers. SMART objectives should be sufficient for most people.

- Effective selection requires more than a tough interview.

Climbing the scaffolding (meetings and recognition)

These two processes come together in this chapter because they are both ongoing and ignored at our peril.

Meetings are a useful part of the scaffolding. They can, on the other hand, go completely awry and cause more problems than they solve. Too many and you find you are having meetings about meetings, the wrong structure and people turn off. Recognition is necessary and nobody would dare argue with that would they?

The basic rules for meetings

- Identify the clear purpose for each type of meeting.
- Regular and short, is better than irregular and lengthy.
- Invite those who need to attend because they have the potential to contribute to a discussion, i.e. they should be part of a two-way communication. If you don't need a discussion just e-mail the information.

We know from the eight-stage circle that we should select the appropriate medium for the message. In my view meetings are for:

- sending messages to the workers en masse that need a) your best interpretation and b) the opportunity for you to check understanding;
- encouraging knowledge sharing;
- encouraging the flow of information and opinions back up the line;
- inclusive decision-making opportunities for two or more people;
- and last, but not least, a mechanism for you to provide support, guidance, a watching brief, delegate etc.

Let's address this last point first as although it is not so instantly obvious as the others, I believe it is the most powerful tool in the box for a middle manager.

One-to-one meetings

Remember my MD's pep talk in Chapter 3? It was along the lines of: 'Right, you have got the job because I think you will do well and you have carte blanche [he almost meant that too!]. If you have any urgent problems or questions come straight in if the door's open. On the other hand we will have fortnightly, diarised meetings when you can keep me updated and we can discuss anything you are unsure of'.

Pretty near perfect in retrospect. I had been bestowed the ultimate level of initiative but he was always in the loop and could spot any excesses on my part before they got out of hand. How to delegate, empower, support, and control in one regular meeting.

In contrast I could name several organisations where the MD only ever managed his managers at formal, monthly, full-scale meetings or on the hoof. The formal meetings brought public criticisms for some managers (not well received) and boredom when their area was not being discussed. The ad hoc meetings were too casual and usually took place when something had gone wrong – so if people saw him coming they usually ducked. Managers rarely went to him with problems because it seemed too big a deal, so they were left to fester.

The regular individual meeting gives us the most effective mechanism to delegate, motivate, spot problems early, and so on. In other words, this is a powerful mechanism to manage individuals and their accountabilities.

There is also a tendency for managers to spend more time with individuals who are working on the stuff we like. If we diarise short meetings with everybody, we are less likely to ignore the difficult or boring issues.

Team meetings

Preferably short and regular; how often depends on the nature of your business but you need them to get two-way communication and knowledge sharing.

Messages from on high must always be interpreted for your audience, so you or your team leaders should be the ones to do this. When you can see people's faces you can tell if they have understood/agreed, and they are more likely to ask you questions than anyone higher up the food chain.

State of the nation addresses from the MD/CEO have their place, but only middle managers can put the messages in true context.

You could decide on one 30-minute weekly meeting to cover all eventualities, or have two different types of meetings further apart. Say, one for overall business issues and another for the tasks in hand.

To summarise, team meetings should cover all of the following but not necessarily all at the same meeting:

- overall business performance
- new initiatives/change
- changes to legislation and impact on us
- general notices/reminders
- new people/leavers
- joint problem-solving/decision-making
- updates on the outside work factors that affect us, e.g. competitors, change in interest rates, market forces (important because it puts things into perspective).

One organisation I know has a more formal management team meeting at the beginning of the week and an informal meeting over tea and buns at the end of the week. 'What are you going to do?' followed by 'well, that was a week, that was', if you like.

Another smaller company has whole organisation pizza meetings every Friday. Each department takes it in turn to organise and set the agenda. Anything can be covered.

Other places have rare team meetings on site but one day and a night away-days every quarter. This suits long-term project-based technical people, whereas 30 minutes every week suits fast-moving, lower-tech people.

Another idea that I have seen used to great effect is loaning one of your experts to another team meeting on a short-term basis (i.e. not always and forever) in order to educate/support – a sort of surgery-based idea. The expert could be there to help sort problems, but ideally, they should be educating before the problems start, and setting up a programme of meetings to minimise the fire-fighting.

Meeting structure

Very little effort is required in meeting structure but for some reason many managers are not prepared to make that effort.

- *One-to-ones* require a common format, which is known to all-comers. For example:
  - Progress on current projects
  - New initiatives
  - Current foreseeable problems.
- *Short frequent team meetings* require variety and spice but no formal agenda.
- *Regular team meetings* with more meat require:
  - An agenda
  - A note of action points to be taken and who will do them
  - Report on action points progress at the start of the next meeting without fail.

If you do not always follow up at the next meeting, promises will be forgotten and actions will slide.

Skills tips for meetings

- Basically the old-fashioned rules for meetings still apply: circulate an agenda in advance, together with papers to be read in advance, chair it properly, minute action points at least, follow up action points at the next meeting. Buy a book on meetings if this is one of your weak spots, anyone can instigate good meeting discipline, you don't have to be gifted.
- Any party line/state of the nation interpretation from you needs to be followed up with *open* questions. 'Does that

make sense?' invariably invites a series of grumpy nods. Whereas 'What do you think of that?' usually provokes some response. 'Which bits don't you agree with?' is not for the faint-hearted, but it is best to get the negatives on the table so they can be discussed.

- Regularly invite constructive communication up the chain, through you. Never pass up negative comments without a positive spin. Remember, going native is seen to be a bad thing.

- Deal with the whingers swiftly and firmly. Whinging is destructive and doesn't even make the whinger feel better. You cannot afford to have more whingers than normal people.

- Always do a real state of the nation address of your own immediately prior to pay review time. Talk about inflation and cost of living but get the facts, not a headline from a tabloid. Talk about growth, what's happening in the marketplace and so on. Cover anything that is related to the topic and that will support your pay decisions generally. Even if you have no input at all in the pay decision, you can still talk about the state of the market, and some constructive feedback for the decision makers would also be useful.

Skills tips for behaviour management

There are plenty of books and courses on this subject so I only intend to cover the key points here that link specifically to meetings.

Your behaviour

- When you lead a meeting you set the tone and influence behaviour just by what you do and set store by. For example, if you are often late or cancel meetings, other people will quickly do the same. If you bang the table and get cross, they will either do the same or clam up. Your behaviour provokes a response, so think on it.

- Ask several people for feedback on your style and what effect they think it has. Resolve to change, preferably publicly at the next meeting if possible. You will not lose face, only gain respect.

Set your standards or ground rules

- Decide what they are and tell the team. Stick to them.

Allow the team to agree their own ground rules

- I always insist on this when things have got out of hand and I have been called in to facilitate, but you don't have to wait till it gets this dire. Point out to them that it's a lot easier to point out an infringement light-heartedly if the ground rules have been agreed in advance.
- Whether you combine this with setting your own ground rules, or allow the team no say in setting the rules, you must be the keeper of the rules. Take suggestions from anyone and ask them all to agree the rules. You will find that others will also point out infringements.

Accept and deal with disagreement

- Disagreements are good, but conflict is a disagreement that has gone too far and affects other people or the work in hand. Accept that disagreements will happen; you shouldn't actively encourage them but you don't want disagreements to remain unsaid and fester.

- Ensure that disagreements are constructive. Protect the weak and sit on the far too strong.

Open challenges

- If you want people to challenge the status quo or even your ideas, make sure that you a) recruit people who can do that and b) set the parameters.

- I have a colleague who tells HR to only send strong people in her direction 'If they are too green, send them to someone else to be nurtured and then we'll see how they are'. She knows that the timid will only get battered by her, and recruits accordingly. Sensible and fair.

- Squashing challenges, or never allowing them in the first place, is counterproductive; this breeds resentment and means you only have one way of doing things – yours.

- The middle course is the safest unless your whole team is rough and tough and we will cover that next.

Involvement and empowerment

We had a client who recognised that she managed a very experienced team and therefore was keen that they manage their own team meetings as well as negotiating among themselves to achieve results. With no supporting structures except an open door policy and a very intelligent, pleasant nature she thought them able to manage their own work. This she said was empowerment. Sadly it was really abdication.

Managers need to manage people and chair meetings, not all the time but actually most of the time. Sorry.

However, you can control the level of input from the team by deciding in advance what is set in stone, up for consultation and what is their decision. It's simple ... just tell them.

This issue is non negotiable, we must implement this because of XYZ (plus some more selling if required). However how we do it is up to us. This is the end result we need (describe it) so any ideas on how we implement this?

Alternatively, 'The end result we are aiming for is ABC. As a team you have carte blanche to design the plan'.

Remember from the introduction to the book – you decide your own leadership style and adjust your actions accordingly.

Influences on decision making in teams

There are two tendencies worth reflecting on here, and I mention them simply because I see them happening at times in front of my very eyes. A manager could easily be powerless to stop these happening.

Risky shift

Stoner (1961) put forward the concept that there is a tendency for groups of people to gamble with decisions more than they would if they were making the decision as an individual alone. This is because together they are more willing to accept uncertainty of the end result. The responsibility for the decision is shared rather than down to one person. The group drives for consensus so they compromise and negotiate. Group leaders believe themselves once removed, and that they will attract hardly any blame from the consequences.

Groupthink

Janis and Mann (1977) identified *Groupthink* in committees and working parties where dissent is considered disloyal, so people are likely to hold back their opposing views. Also the group is over optimistic about the outcomes.

So what does this mean for you?

Set the parameters for the team by clearly agreeing the desired outcomes up-front, e.g. strategic aims? In line with overall objectives?

Don't allow compromise just to stop feelings getting hurt. Construct a logical step-by-step plan, take into account contingencies but don't allow the focus to be lost.

Reward and recognition

This topic is covered here because how you reward and recognise good performance has to be a combination of processes that you actively select up front. Praise and reward cannot be activities that you do when you have time or because the organisation demands it.

The best managers have thought this one through and have an active, ongoing strategy.

It is, of course, one of the grand debates guaranteed to generate opinions from the quietest people. It's quite simple really – we all need praise and we all want to be valued for what we bring to the party. And preferably we would like financial reward for what we are worth (that one is always the hot potato and better brains than ours argue about it).

So, in my mind, it is better to stick to the facts and reality as it is today in the UK in the twenty-first century. You can try to buck the system, and indeed you should if you can justify it, but that's a point for later. What matters, however, is quite simple.

What's the point?

Reward and recognition processes should be designed to fulfil the following functions:

- Reinforcing personal feeling of 'worth' by honestly and proactively valuing successes.

- Reinforcing 'the way we do things round here', e.g. if teamwork or creativity are high on your list recognise them when you see them.

- Encouraging more of the good stuff and none of the bad or mediocre.

- Valuing diversity of expertise by making sure you recognise different strengths (more on this later – we can't all be good at everything).

- Reward the engine room as well as the stars – everyone on the bridge and no-one in the engine room would grind all of us to a halt.

Many large organisations go in for fancy, athletic recognition schemes and if you work for one of those, good luck to you. It means you have more choices, and possible more chances of tripping up.

Many organisations have robust pay schemes with scope to financially reward success. Now that's really useful, if you belong to one of those use your power wisely and everyone will benefit.

Living with reward realities

- *Reality*: Whatever you have in place in your organisation that is outside your control, live with it, try to bend it when you can, but concentrate on your own area.

- *Reality*: Actions and words mean everything, money has a limited effect on performance (stay calm here).

- *Reality*: Market rate governs pay and that's a fact. Accept it and move on.

- *Reality*: No one else looks hard at market rates so you should make it your business, constantly; never take your eye off the ball because the market does shift. HR should make a reasonable fist of watching market rates but only you know what your people do compared with the job on offer. Get the data and make your case if you think your people should be paid more. They will adore you, but not forever.

OK so let's get back to the everyday, common or garden scaffolding. For start let's merge the words 'reward and recognition' and look at a pick 'n' mix of actions that 'value good performance'. Actions that you select might be words, they might be money, they might be gifts, maybe even more work. It's up to you to choose what's best for your team.

But before we look at the list, think carefully about what you are recognising. I once had a precious team of girls that asked for a lot of thank yous and wanted smiles in the morning and smiles every night, along with the thank yous. I was young and I played the game until my face ached. Switching from that to personal congratulations for achievements won me far more friends and some good financial results. Truly.

Recognition is for:

- work that exceeds expectations;
- solutions to problems that most people cannot solve;
- off-the-wall ideas that have a chance of success;
- determination and grit in the face of adversity;

- improvements to performance that are entirely self-made, however small;

- extra effort beyond the call of duty.

Recognition is not for:

- just doing the job you are paid to do – it's a contract for services, they do the work and you pay them for it;

- somebody else's efforts or ideas.

We will get to the pick 'n' mix shortly but one last thought. You do not have to go with the flow – be creative and pick recognition to suit your team. Maybe do something new for a while, try things out, you never know until you try.

Pick 'n' mix recognition actions

The absolute must haves:

- *Verbal praise.* Praise should be direct to the individual, straight away. And make it specific, not just 'well done' but 'that report was concise and to the point, it made an impact on Fred'.

- *Go out of your way to find the person and praise them.* Find them at their desk or wherever they work. Don't wait till they come to you for some other reason; the praise will look like an afterthought.

- *Praise them publicly.* Use public praise whenever you can, ideally at a meeting in front of the rest of the team, or other teams.

- *Pass on external praise.* Any praise that comes from outside the team should be passed on to the recipient straight away, or saved for public praise at a meeting. Say who said it and why, and then say why it's important to you.

- *Seek out customer praise.* Pass it on to the right person/people. Both this and the last type of praise should be for general knowledge – remember this is specifying the sort of performance that you want more of.
- *Recognise expertise.* Most people have strengths or expertise that others could learn from, even if the recipients never get to be as good as the expert. If you can, get the experts to coach others or at least pass on tips or advice. When you ask the expert to embark on this coaching tell them why you want them to do it – because they are good, really good in that area.

  In reality, of course, some experts are hopeless at coaching others. In that case perhaps they could write a report or a training checklist or speak for a few minutes at a meeting. You may need to be imaginative here. At the end of the day, the passing on of expertise is a good enough reason to engage the expert but the principal benefit is that they know you value their strengths.

- *Specific public recognition.* Whether it's in newsletters or on the intranet, recognition should be precise – painting a very clear picture of what was precisely excellent in their performance. A rotating 'employee of the month' simply will not do.

When talking to different managers from different organisations, they all agreed that the above pick 'n' mix points were spot on. Even if they did not always do each point themselves, they usually resolved to try harder. The next selection of pick 'n' mix caused controversy; from 'Yes I have done that and it works' to 'Oh no, that wouldn't possibly work in my organisation!'. The latter was usually said by a manager who had never tried it at all. So just think about it carefully before you reject it out of hand. Remember the Quality Street or Roses tin after Christmas – in some houses all the toffees are left, in others all the coffee creams. So some teams respond well to one type of recognition and well ... just don't give out coffee creams.

- *Pots of gold.* A sum of money under your direct control for you to do with as you wish. Usually spent on a gift tailor-made for the recipient; quality lipstick, Haynes manual for an MGB, basket of exotic fruit for someone on a diet and so on – whatever is personal and appropriate at the time. Something that makes them realise you and/or the team have put thought into it. And that's the point, it *is* the thought that counts.

  Of course, you may not have been allocated a pot of gold, but if it's possible and legal, argue for one or siphon off a chunk from the training budget. After all, this is team development at its most sophisticated.

  You should set the criteria for the pot of gold but the team could decide on an ad hoc basis who gets a reward. (Don't ever do it regularly, e.g. on the first of each month – it will lose credibility before the year is out.) Whoever decides, just make sure that everyone knows what it's for: something over and above the call of duty.

  I did once get charming, professional service from a very scary looking 'backroom' man, and duly passed on my compliments to the manager. The porter had been kept in the back for sometime out of harm's way (on both sides) but this was a breakthrough so he received his first ever pot of gold and has stepped up a gear.

- *Team rewards.* These can range from general jolly outings (appropriate to *your* team), structured team building days, acquiring new skills, to voluntary work. The jolly outings are usually more effective for teams who achieve a certain record, e.g. highest percentage increase in profitability (every team stands a chance then). The other types of days are for everyone and really are not a reward – they belong in the team development chapter.

- *Fancy recognition schemes.* Several large organisations have these in place with managers nominating recipients who can then choose from sophisticated menus. I have no idea whether they are valued by the workplace or not, however if you don't have such a scheme in your organisation, do not fret, there are other ways.

- *Monthly bottles of champagne.* Once again, anything on a monthly basis loses its value. Spend the money on something else.

- *Incentives vs. rewards.* What is an incentive and what's a reward? It's a big debate, but not relevant here. Sales people like to be rewarded for results, so do it if it fits your culture. Other employees are less impressed – they want to be rewarded in their pay. So better spend time here arguing for a merit pay system.

- *Bonuses for hitting targets.* These have become popular in the last 10 years as companies have bought more into setting objectives and then paying out one-off bonuses if they are achieved at the year end. There may well be research showing this works but cynics say it's just a way of *not* increasing the pay and pension bill year on year. Many employees, however, value their self-worth on what they are paid in comparison with others, so for our purposes we should consider chunky bonuses as valuable recognition of efforts. Of course, the whole shooting match depends on the quality of the original objectives.

- *Good suggestion bonuses.* Again many organisations have a bonus system for ideas with bottom-line business impact. The rewards can be in the hundreds or thousands of pounds, often depending on actual business impact. Even if your organisation does not have a scheme set up there is nothing to stop you making a financial case on behalf of one of your employees. Indeed you should, as it will be an all round 'win' situation.

- *Extra time off.* Giving an employee extra time off when they want it, for all-round extra effort, is a powerful and low-cost piece of recognition. The proviso here is that you must be able to justify it in the broader scheme of things; HR managers can get very jittery here if you hand it out wantonly. But if people give you extra, over and above the contract, in my view it is fair to give back. For some, indeed a lot of, people, extra time when they need it is worth more than money or gifts.

- *'Feel good' gifts.* One CEO I knew was admired by a lot of people for always buying every employee an Easter egg out of his own purse. This is not specific recognition so has limited value but the effects should not be underestimated. Lateral thinking is important here in order to recognise, and promote, diversity so think through other festival gifts. If you have a truly multi-cultural team it might get expensive though so you could go back to basics and simply buy ice cream cones (with chocolate sticks) in the summer. Even if you don't have a policy for feel good gifts you could still splash out on a rare occasion; everyone might wonder what you are up to but it will be remembered.

Scaffolding summary

Debates go on all the time about reward and recognition and there are some very sophisticated systems around.

The concepts are all about

- Reinforcing personal worth – showing people you value what they do/have done.
- Reinforcing 'the way we do things round here'.
- Encouraging more of the same 'good behaviour'.
- Showing other people openly that that is the sort of stuff you want from them.
- Showing you value experts in *different* skills.

Your actions have got to be

- Specific.
- Worth something.
- Different companies vary in what they think is good or gimmicky – try not to get stuck in a rut from the past, be prepared to try things differently.
- At the same time be consistent with *your* praise and reward otherwise everyone gets confused.

5

Feedback on the construction (monitor and review people's progress)

The bad news is that managing performance is a big and complex subject; the good news is that you have already covered by far the hardest parts. The groundwork in the first three chapters gives you the solid foundations and the bulk of the processes you need for performance management. All that remains is monitoring and reviewing progress (here in Chapter 5) and development (Chapter 6).

Here we assess processes to:

- Step 1: Monitor work yourself and through others.
- Step 2: Assess the data you collect.
- Step 3: Feedback to the individual informally and formally.
- Step 4: Deal with under-performance.

All these bits of scaffolding are designed to look for improvements in effectiveness and development in skills and, as usual, must join up with strategic goals and other processes.

Step 1: Monitoring work

We have already looked at competencies, objectives, performance standards, and tools such as balanced scorecards and RAG reports. All, or a combination of any, of these will give you data; this achieved, that not. However, let's look at the simplest methods that give more qualitative information.

Managing by walking about

Managing by walking about (MBWA) is the simplest piece of scaffolding and all the best managers do it. Get out of your zone/desk area and walk about once a day or a week at least. 'How's X going?', 'Any problems with Y?'. Specific questions get you started and are considered appropriate from the manager. General questions just get general answers and tend to make people suspicious of your motives.

After the specifics you can move on to linked, general questions such as 'So how do you find X department generally to deal with?', 'What are customers saying about Y?'

While you are there look at the state of their desk, watch their facial expressions; basically gather the underlying messages.

Listen as you go round; *what* is being said and *how* will give you lots of clues. Listen in the lunch queue, listen before meetings start.

Ask others

Ask consultants, trainers, other managers, 'How is X project progressing?', 'What else could we do for you about that?'.

These questions prompt positive, constructive answers. Of course some of those questioned only want to whinge, or simply cannot think constructively, but asking others will still give more clues. Try and pin the whingers down to suggesting constructive solutions, it will be good for their own development and shows you do not want, and will not tolerate, moaning about your people.

Initiate review meetings – short, sweet and focused – anything less will aggravate others. The best managers do this regularly; they are seen as the people who are proactive in solving issues. If you are constructive in these there will be good quality feedback available about your team.

Ask the other stakeholders: customers, investors, suppliers and so on. I have seen some terribly constructed surveys, but that is no reason to dismiss them. They give you good headline data if the questions are phrased appropriately (so engage an expert).

A construction company we have worked with always sent in a senior manager to interview the client at the end of the project. Expectations were pinned down at the outset of the project and questions asked at the end. Take some care here because this company found that the client only commented on the final six weeks and had to be interrogated (nicely of course) about the remaining 50 weeks. Even so, eyeball to eyeball interviews give you a mass of information. Press for their perceptions and why, get quotes.

Ask your team leaders

Absolutely crucial – they should have sharp-end knowledge and know more about motives and habits than anyone. If they do not have good quality information to give you, it's probably time to train them.

Step 2: Assess the data you collect

You will have quants and quals (quantative and qualitative data). Remember lies, dammed lies and statistics though. You must interpret.

Look for underlying reasons

If an objective is not achieved it could be down to poor resources or support. Maybe your delegation techniques need revamping. Perhaps priorities went askew. Maybe customers are changing their habits. Whatever, investigate the cause and effect. You see the effects but what are the causes?

What can be done to resolve causes?

If you map out the causes and effects you should be able to identify what could be done to resolve problems. Is it a major strategic issue, micro-strategic, or down to one person's idiotic actions?

Just don't take things on face value, that's all I'm saying.

Ask the team

If after reviewing the data it would appear that this is not down to an individual, present the data to the team and seek their views. However, before you do this, get your ducks in a row.

- What do *you* perceive are the causes? Is it down to you personally?
- What can/can't be changed?
- What resources might be needed and what are available?
- What standards do you ultimately want to aim for?
- What might the costs be?

It is vital you are well-prepared but open-minded. Not easy that, I know, but there is always more than one way to skin a cat. Remember, present the situation, with the non-negotiables clearly stated up front, and ask for solutions (various problem-solving textbooks will be of use here).

Skills tips

- Pay attention when you are listening – look people in the eye, ask follow-up questions and summarise back what you think you have understood, 'So what you are saying is this ...'. People will go off you if you don't listen properly and get the wrong end of the stick – it's a fact.

- Pick appropriate times, be direct but calm and pleasant. People on the back foot never give coherent replies that get to the heart of the matter.

- Test 'shopping surveys' are useful for information on a moment in time, and if you do them regularly they will show trends. They don't have to be expensive – you could use internal experts to ring up (face-to-face they are very likely to be spotted).

Step 3: Providing feedback

The performance review should not be an annual event; monitoring and reviewing should take place regularly throughout the year especially as the current work climate for most people involves change. The skills outlined in this section are the same for regular, informal reviews as well as the annual review.

Of course there is great responsibility for management to ensure that people receive the right support and resources to achieve their objectives throughout the year, and part of this is the way we managers actually manage.

Self-assessment

We all should be encouraged to review and reflect on our own performance. For a formal performance review an organisation often uses a structured form to encourage reflection, which will then be used as a basis for the discussion. But during the course of the year it is up to the manager to set the tone for the self-assessment and resulting discussion by asking open questions.

Having clearly defined individual objectives makes this conversation constructive and a regular review of objectives, known to the employee, prompts self assessment.

Sample questions:

- How are you progressing overall?
- How are you getting on with xxx objective?
- What are the problems?
- How did you deal with them?
- What drew you to that conclusion?
- What have you learned from that experience?
- What would you do differently next time?

The advantages of the self-assessment approach are that:

- Individuals are encouraged to review themselves, not wait for it to be 'done' to them.
- It promotes the right sort of learning culture.
- It promotes quality self reflection.
- If we offer weaknesses and solutions ourselves the manager will not need to make a deal of it.

Skills tips

The overall aim of any performance discussion is to reach agreement on the way forward.

Self-assessment forms are often used prior to formal performance reviews. In my view they should not be completed and given to the manager in advance of the discussion because that puts all the cards in your hands (unfair). Besides, if you are any good you should know most of it.

Performance reviews

Remember to review achievable performance: individual efforts are limited by other people, resources, time, information flows etc. When you prepare for the review as a manager you should have thoroughly researched the individual's performance and have examples ready to demonstrate clearly what you mean.

- Ensure that regular reviews take place, within set timescales.
- Tackle issues as they arise, no nasty surprises to be saved up for review time.
- Check that you both understand the individual's role and objectives.
- Recognise success and address underperformance.
- Clarify the role of individuals for a specified period following the review.
- Agree objectives and operating practices. Make sure that the person understands what is required of them.
- Make sure that all ratings (if given) are consistent and fair.
- Make sure that all observations can be substantiated.

- Take action to develop people to achieve the job requirements and beyond if it is appropriate, by coaching, support and formal training where necessary.

- Create a climate where a performance review system can operate effectively.

- Request feedback from the individual being reviewed.

The objectives set for the individual will form the basis of the next review:

- What has been achieved?

- How was it achieved?

- Was it completed within the agreed timescale?

- Were there any missed opportunities?

- Are there any future opportunities that can be addressed?

Other issues to consider

- Linking pay to performance reviews – if you do not discuss pay at appraisals make sure you set aside another time to do so.

- Torrington and Hall (1991) suggest that managers need to think carefully about the primary purpose of their appraisal system. There are many options, e.g. improve current performance, provide feedback, increase motivation, identify training needs, identify potential, let individuals know what is expected of them, focus on career development, award salary increases and solve job problems. If you try to cover all of these, the review will become complex. Stick to the main theme – agreeing to move forward.

- 360-degree feedback – more commonly used these days with online tools available. Make sure you give feedback in the same constructive way. Don't just give them the report to read.

Figure 5.1 provides a simple, generic view of performance reviews.

Figure 5.1 A simple, generic view of performance reviews

Generic view of performance reviews

Clarify organisational goals and measurements of success

Strategic tool

Identify team and individual objectives

(Include performance standards)

Review team and individual objectives regularly

The annual performance review

Step back, holistic review of performance, hopes and opportunities

Agree the way forward

Agree development objectives

The appraisal process

1. Preparation

   - Plan the place, time and environment.
   - Review the individual's performance history and encourage them to do the same. Consult others if necessary.
   - Allow time to prepare.

2. Discussion

   - Clarify your understanding of the job role (both of you).
   - Ask questions and listen. Encourage the individual to talk.
   - Praise where it's due; recognise achievements.
   - Discuss, don't argue.
   - Identify problems and solutions. Be fair.

3. Agreement

   - Joint problem-solving to gain commitment.
   - Agree an action plan with clear responsibilities (yours, theirs).
   - Get the individual to summarise to check understanding.

4. Report

   - Complete the form after the discussion.
   - Encourage the employee to comment.

5. Follow-up

   - Plan the agreed action and carry it out.
   - Monitor progress.
   - Keep communicating with the individual.

Review styles

Of course an organisation can have the most logical and efficient review process in the world but the success of the discussion will depend entirely upon the reviewer's style. Maier (1958) describes the choices we have and the impact on the quality of the discussion as *Telling, Telling and selling, Telling and listening and Sharing.* Remember the overall aim of the discussion is to agree how the reviewee will move forward. The old-fashioned autocratic style does not achieve agreement at all, not even a willingness to adapt; it's more like handing down a judgment from on high and most people resent that style.

The most commonly used styles these days is sharing; it involves lots of open questions, listening, the 80/20 rule – you talk 20 per cent of the time, the reviewee talks 80 per cent of the time, and a joint approach to developing performance. A one-day course in conducting effective review discussions would give you all the skills you need.

Remember though that if you are a routinely autocratic manager, but try the sharing approach at review time, your employees will find you a tad schizophrenic and will probably remain fairly quiet. There is also another style not even shown on the scale – the leave well alone approach. In other words not dealing with any weaknesses or areas for development, just saying nice things. Needless to say, this style gets you nowhere except eventually backwards, and is fraught with difficulties for both of you.

1. *Telling.* Autocratic, only works if you command vast respect and they are not allowed to have a mind of their own.

2. *Telling and selling.* Might work initially but any resentment or disbelief will eventually surface.

3. *Telling and listening.* You go first and listen hard. By actively involving them you are more likely to get a positive response.

4. *Sharing.* Joint problem solving. Harder to plan but a good investment of time.

Agreeing and monitoring team and individual action plans

An action plan should be drawn up following the review. It should specify what needs to be done, by whom, how and to what timescale.

The focus should be short and long term. It should contain details of:

- agreed development needs of the team or individual;
- what the outcomes of the development activities will be;
- those individuals with responsibility for the development activity and the role they will play;
- details of the support needed for the individual or team to carry out the development activity; this may involve the manager, HR or trainers;
- if appropriate, how the development activity will be measured;
- time frames.

Some action plans are highly structured detailing exact competencies and level of skill required. Others are informal. Research by Armstrong and Baron (1998) reveals that the majority of organisations have a moderate amount of structure in their post-review action plans, covering basic details of the development activity, expected outcomes, the support needed and the timing.

What happens between performance reviews?

Continuous monitoring and review of both the team and the individual's performance needs to take place throughout the year.

> Leaving team dynamics to manage performance by such things as team pressure can be dangerous and unfair. Managing team performance is important, but it is not a substitute for managing individual performance. (Wright and Barding, 1992)

Step 4: Dealing with underperformance

Starting point

If you have agreed SMART objectives and regular review systems then it should be very clear when an individual is underperforming. However, it is essential to look beyond the symptoms of underperformance and dig to find the causes.

We also should work to the assumption that underperformance can be improved. After all, it is rare for people to come to work to deliberately do a bad job. It is best for the manager's conscience, the benefit of the employee and to comply with legal requirements that we put every effort into helping a person improve.

Causes of underperformance

- Confusion about the job – lack of clarity.
- Inability to do the job – lack of skills, knowledge.

- Poor attitude or motivation – may result in a lack of effort or self-discipline.

- Obstacles at work – poor job design, faulty equipment, understaffing etc.

- Non-work factors – health, home, bereavement etc.

- Anxiety, bullying, cultural conflict, illness, stress, substance abuse, financial problems, depression.

Six-step plan for dealing with underperformance

1. Identify the cause, collect relevant evidence.

2. Identify how the issue should be addressed – change objectives only if they are unrealistic, change plans on how to achieve the objectives if appropriate.

3. Agree and record action. Set clear timescales and stick to them.

4. Meet to review progress. Keep to the timetable and record the outcomes of meetings.

5. Deal with continued underperformance and be prepared to take disciplinary action if necessary.

6. Don't save things up for the review. Tackle issues as they arise.

Scaffolding summary

- Feedback processes are vital: we might design a superb set of scaffolding but unless we recognise that feedback has to be regular and effective then the whole structure stays static, and eventually crumbles.

- These processes are fundamental but you do not have to rely on direction from on high. No performance review systems? Then design a simple one just for your department.

- All the other processes you have in place give you plenty of opportunities for monitoring work and giving feedback. Use them all the time.

- Dealing with underperformance must be done for your sake and theirs. Imagine what it might be like after 10 years in a job to find yourself considered not good enough or stuck in a rut. A manager's first obligation is to keep people moving forward, the second is constructive honesty. People need to know where they stand so that they can be in control of their own destiny. A lack of constructive honesty is just plain mean.

6

Improving the structure (help people develop)

By now, it is a generally accepted fact that developing employees is a good thing to do. Having said that I do occasionally come across some organisations who see no point, or have not got the time, or believe their employees are fine as they are, or say they have no money. Well, we are all flat out and development does not have to cost hard cash. It is essential, in my view, not only to keep people up-to-date but to stretch and move them forward.

Remember the PESTLE factors in Chapter 1?

All types of change have implications for workforce development, which is a key factor in enabling the organisation to:

- respond effectively to changes in the environment;
- keep ahead of the competition;
- promote a high performance culture.

For the organisation, failure to anticipate and respond to change may result in loss of markets, customers, revenue, or independence.

Another, more simple, reason is that we do not all have the knowledge, skills or attitude (KSA) to perform the job role well. There are often gaps in competencies to be addressed.

Therefore, we will consider, in this chapter, the steps to setting up basic scaffolding for employee development.

- Step 1: Start with the strategy
- Step 2: Team and individual plans
- Step 3: Development solutions
- Step 4: Evaluation

Step 1: Start with the strategy

Why develop the workforce?

As you would expect by now, you will need to revisit the organisation's purpose and your micro-strategy. But the good news is that you already have those in place. Figure 6.1 shows that if you know where you are going, you can analyse any gaps in knowledge, skills and attitude and plan how to deliver and implement solutions.

For example, if your micro-strategy is to improve customer service or increase efficiency you will need to assess the knowledge, skills and attitudes of your team in relation to those aspects. So:

- What are your goals?
- What tasks must be completed to achieve those goals?
- What behaviours are necessary for each job holder to complete their tasks?
- What deficiencies, if any, do job holders have in knowledge, skills or attitudes required to perform the necessary behaviours? (Robbins 1978)

The outcome will be the *development gap* (Figure 6.2: CRC, 2005).

Figure 6.1 Why develop the workforce

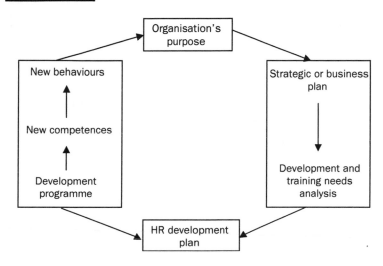

Figure 6.2 The development gap

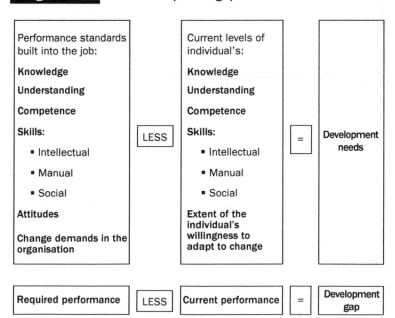

You may even properly consider using your micro-strategy headings to lead the training needs analysis. This approach ensures that you focus on the priorities but leave nothing out. Remember though to think laterally with the headings and deeper into the behaviours required; a micro-strategy including customer focus and efficiency might not, for example, instantly reveal Fred's poor time management. We will look briefly at a more scientific approach to individual training needs analysis later. At this point just think collectively about the team and the micro-strategy.

Skills tips

The climate

Think about your department's attitude to development. What sort of culture exists and what attitude do you actively encourage? Think about:

- How *you* react to mistakes?
- Is there a blame culture?
- Is risk-taking encouraged?
- Do people help each other learn?

In other words, do you use other bits of scaffolding to encourage a learning environment?

Your attitude to learning in general will shape your team's attitude to 'task' learning and ultimately the general attitude to development.

It will be very hard to develop skills and attitudes if you have a poor climate. Some people will react badly, even behave badly when training comes along in a poor climate. And the point is that the climate in your department is set by you, never mind what else is going on in the rest of the organisation.

The solution

Set an example; show *you* can learn constructively from mistakes and risk-taking.

- Don't blame others, even if it is their fault; look for positive actions to take to resolve issues.

- Start development off with quick, simple interventions such as pairing up an expert with a learner on a specific issue, or organising a good quality internal training session (short and punchy) that will hit the mark instantly. Do not choose a conceptual subject, pick a practical or extremely interesting training need to address.

- Put real effort into analysing the development need and finding a tailored solution. Avoid simple courses that everyone has to attend whether they need them or not.

- Use praise as a process to encourage positive attitudes to learning. Give public, constructive praise to people who share knowledge or help others learn.

Step 2: Team and individual plans

Many people use the words 'development' and 'training' as if they were synonymous. In fact they have rather different meanings.

Development refers to the whole process of realising a person's full potential, and therefore applies to personal as well as professional life. It also refers to a range of interventions.

Training, on the other hand, is a focused development method, which helps people to acquire certain job-related knowledge, skills and/or attitudes.

Stages in the development process

At its most basic the development process has four main stages:

- analysing the priority development needs of the organisation, teams and individuals;
- planning a development programme for individuals and groups;
- implementing the development programme;
- evaluating the effectiveness of the programme to see if the learning has taken place and the benefits it has produced.

Training needs analysis

Boydell (1983) suggests that training needs can exist at three levels:

- *Organisational:* priorities, culture, change etc.
- *Job or occupational:* groups needing to improve performance.
- *Individual:* skills, knowledge, attitudes.

This means that any thorough review of development needs should start with an organisational review, although there may be other specific triggers which initiate a review such as:

- establishment of a training function and budget;
- for corporate planning and longer-term training needs;
- a major change in an organisation's activities;
- requests from management: to meet a new problem or a growing awareness of issues;
- to meet a national standard, e.g. IiP, ISO;

- ensure that statutory requirements are met: e.g. health and safety, discrimination legislation.

Barrington and Reid (1994) suggest there are four steps in identifying organisational needs:

- preparation – clear brief, inform people, advance notice for information;
- collect data and interpret (see Table 6.1);
- interpret data, determine key areas, develop recommendations;
- prepare to implement.

However when you come to consider planning development you will need to have the answers to the following questions (CRC, 2005). Ask yourself:

1. *The performance problem.* What is or is not happening? Who is doing or not doing what? What are the effects of the problem?

Table 6.1   Where to collect data and for what

Where to collect data from	To find out?
Planning documents	Marketing, staffing production plans
Minutes of management meetings	Any clues about the future
HR statistics	Absence or labour turnover figures and reasons
Accident records	Causes of accidents
Performance reviews	Individual needs
Financial data	Waste figures
Interviews with key people	Goals not down on paper
Surveys	Customer or employee views
Directly observing work	What you see is what you get

2. *Ownership*. Who really owns this problem? Does it belong to you or your department alone? Is employee development the correct answer to the problem?

3. *The ideal solution*. Imagine the problem has been solved; what is the ideal situation that would result and what would it achieve?

4. *The evidence for success*. What would you observe (i.e. what would people do or say) that would prove that the problem had been successfully solved?

5. *Potential losses*. If you succeed, might there be unexpected losses as well as gains?

6. *The development gap*. What is the gap between the present and ideal solution?

7. *The difficulties*. What is currently preventing you or your department from getting to the ideal?

8. *The context*. When, where and with whom do you want to achieve this ideal? Who or what else needs to be involved?

9. *The resources*. What resources do you need? What do you have already? What extra do you want? Who can supply them?

10. *The strategy*. How are you going to get from A to B? What are the key stages along the way? What do you need to do to ensure progress is made?

This 10-step plan is a good starting point before you embark on a full-blown training exercise. You may find at Step 2 that this is not a training problem at all. For example, an employee's apparently poor time management may be purely down to not being able to delegate. Coaching from you may be more appropriate. If, however, there appears to be a training need, the first stage is to analyse the task itself.

Task analysis

To find out the training needs, there are various approaches available all around job analysis in the first instance. As Boydell (1977) points out 'Job analysis is a process of examining a job. Thus it is not a particular document, but rather gives rise to certain documents, the product of an analytical examination of the job'.

Types of analysis

- *Comprehensive*: all facets of the job task analysis – core parts of the job.

- *Problem centred*: focusing only on an area for concern, e.g. report writing.

We will concentrate on the task analysis but it is important not to keep the scope too narrow as we may find that we have missed an important part of the development gap. For example, analysis around the key task area of presentation skills for an account manager may miss the proactive approach to:

- keeping up-to-date with product knowledge
- internal networking
- converting presentations to sales etc.

Sources of information to prepare the task analysis

- *Written*: Job descriptions, appraisals, questionnaires.
- *Oral*: Observation and questions, ask other experts and departments.

Each job will have:

- *Skills*: diagnostic, decision-making, interpersonal, etc.

- *Knowledge*: technical, procedural, etc.

- *Attitudes*: courtesy, flexibility, calmness, etc.

- *Competence*: degree of capability to perform each task.

A training or HR expert would help you prepare and write a job analysis that defines exactly the task, knowledge, skills and attitudes required. However, I am suggesting that, although thorough, it is not necessary for your purposes.

Instead you have two choices:

1. Rely on your good sense and knowledge to be able to clearly define aims and objectives for any development you plan. Write the objectives down and ensure they are SMART.

2. Put together a self-assessed skills profile (see, for example, Panel 6.1). This has several benefits:

   - You prepare the definitive list of KSAs for an aspect of a job role that you believe people need training in.

   - It's not a whole job analysis – just the aspect of the job you want to focus on, and therefore not too arduous.

   - It can blend KSAs into simple statements that people can easily interpret.

   - It will provide the basis of any development activity you choose.

   - Individuals can self assess against the profile before development, which will show the gaps to address (or you can assess if you don't think they will be honest).

   - Individuals can self assess after the training, which will show the improvement (or you can).

Panel 6.1 Chairing meetings: self assessed skills profile

Scoring

0 = I never do this
1 = I sometimes to do this
2 = I often do this
3 = I always do this

	0	1	2	3
I begin each meeting at its scheduled start time				
I ensure that participants understand the minutes of the previous meeting				
I follow the approved agenda for each meeting				
I explain the purpose of each meeting clearly to all participants				
I allow all points of view to have a fair hearing				
I am aware of each participants motives and hidden agendas				
I ensure that all participants are fully involved in each meeting				
I make sure that I am thoroughly prepared for each meeting				
I refer to a meetings procedure guide before each formal meeting				
I make sure that full and accurate minutes of each meeting are taken				
I ensure that participants know what action to take before the next meeting				
I ensure that participants know the time and place of the next meeting				

- The improvements can be shown as statistics, e.g. 100 per cent of the delegates improved in 80 per cent of the skills.

At its most simple, planning for development is about:

- defining where you are now
- where you want to be
- how you are going to get there
- and, what is often forgotten, how you will know that you have arrived!

The ten steps we have covered before help you define where you are now, the next step is analyse the performance gap, and then you are able to specify where you want to be in terms of the outcomes you expect from the development programme.

Getting from A to B: aims and objectives

An aim gives a general statement of what development you intend to plan. Aims tell you and the learner the general direction in which you are travelling.

Objectives are more precise statements about what the learner will be able to do at the end and should be written in SMART terms. They are useful also to define stages on the way to achieving a goal and in providing benchmarks against which learners' progress can be assessed.

The training plans

Team plans

A well-used option here is to design a large matrix or chart with all the names down one side and all the skills along the top. In each box mark the due completion date. You could even colour code it so the trainer is identified, e.g. Flossie is doing all the training on Excel so all those completion dates are marked in pink for Flossie and so on.

Put it up on the wall and charge the team with ownership from making the training happen all the way through to ticking when done.

Individual plans

These can be as simple or as sophisticated as you like. The minimum should look like this:

- Name:
- Aims:
- Objectives:

    1.

    2.

    3.

    4.

- How I will achieve this and when:
- What support I will need:

Some organisations go in for personal development plans for every employee, others only consider using them for people on long-term development programmes or specific job groups. It must depend on your culture. A young organisation with career-minded people in the main will find it easy to include personal development plans (PDPs) as routine scaffolding, often referred to and updated.

On the other hand PDPs become a joke if they are not 'used', i.e. not referred to from one year to the next. They are definitely worth creating at least once a year, but just make sure *you* refer to them and see that action is taken. If you can't do that, don't bother.

Even if your team is not made up primarily of career-minded thrusting young things, PDPs are worth having as scaffolding because they focus everybody's minds on what is to be developed and how. Indeed, they are an effective process for getting buy-in from individuals on personal development. A catering department might have, for example, many people who the manager believes to be lacking in aspiration, but it is still a good idea to instigate PDPs. Put down the 'hard skills/knowledge' (food hygiene, health and safety etc) and add in at least one 'softer' skill, e.g. team-working, or training others. The staff will know exactly what they should be working on, they have evidence of a training record (for other employers if they move on) and the manager may very well be surprised to find that they have more people interested in learning than they thought.

Skills tip

Continuous Professional Development (CPD) is not a concept reserved for the professions. True, surveyors, accountants, and HR managers are required to undergo regular training to update their skills, and will be spot-checked by their relevant governing bodies from time to time. However, any manager should consider a planned approach to ongoing development and therefore recording it is a good idea.

Good managers think through, at least once a year, what they need to learn, how and when. It does not stop them seizing the moment and adding in extra development on the way.

Step 3: Development solutions

Sending someone on a training course is not the only solution, and not always the best. There are many options. Choose the most effective, not the easiest or cheapest. Think about the individual and how they like to learn, consider the expertise (potential trainers) that you have around you.

Bad managers see training courses as a pill that someone else will administer, and then the individual will return cured. The truth is that a course might help them see the light or understand the theory, but only excellent courses give individuals direct, practical advice on how to start doing something better.

The range of different development methods are compared in Table 6.2. Each have a role to play depending on the culture of the organisation, the motivation and learning styles of the learner and finally, practicalities.

Skills tip

I previously mentioned learning styles briefly. Go to *www.peterhoney.co.uk* to find out your preferred learning style. For example, sending someone who learns well from books on a role-playing course will not work.

Step 4: Evaluation

Why is training and development so frequently not evaluated?

The benefits are often intangible; effectiveness may improve, but in ways that are not immediately obvious. Development activities help an individual to grow, to improve their judgment, and to increase their value to their employer. Such skills develop gradually and may not be suddenly apparent on completion of activities.

Table 6.2 Comparing development methods

Method	Comments
Internal training courses	Cost effective. Ought to be easy to meet training needs and evaluate success. Pick a good trainer.
External training courses	More expensive but mixing with other organisations might be beneficial. The trainer might not be able to give direct practical advice on how to put learning into practice in your unique organisation.
Distance/open learning	Work books and self study can be good, but the learner has to be self-motivated. Only gets done in home time.
e-learning/CBT	Any learning over the Internet or on the computer. Suits some subjects and some people very well. Not good for soft skills in my opinion.
Coaching	Good coaches make a huge impact on putting learning into practice. One to one and very focused. Time consuming but ultimately effective.
Mentor	Mentors cannot be allocated – they have to fit with the individual, command respect and offer stretching sound advice.
Projects	Very good for stretching and learning. Make sure people get off on the right foot and keep a close eye on their progress. Make sure that the project is feasible and has a chance of implementation. People get very disappointed if they invest effort in work that gets ignored.
Attachments	Working somewhere else in the same organisation is beneficial as long as the learner has a proper job to do.
Secondments	Working in another organisation: for example, many large organisations encourage managers to work for free in charities to broaden their exposure and make their own skills useful to others. Good for personal growth if you choose the right organisation.
Competence based development	NVQs are lengthy and require huge amounts of paper based evidence. In my view good for practical subjects like plumbing and hairdressing, but not management unless you are after the qualification rather than development.
Sitting by Nellie	Showing someone what to do, letting them do it and supervising. The best way to learn a whole heap of tasks. Make sure Nellie is good at explaining.

Even where measurable change exists it is not always easy to establish a direct link between the training and the results because there are many other influencing factors.

The result is that evaluation is often confined to questionnaires completed by the trainees at the end of the training (what we call happiness sheets). Courses are not the only development activity, but even so, there are reasons to be cautious in attaching too much importance to such questionnaires. Easterby-Smith and Tanton (1985) point out three drawbacks:

- Evaluations can be conservative – danger of adverse criticism reflecting on the trainee or the trainer or the continuation of the course.

- Evaluations can be counterproductive because they focus on what the trainee wants rather than what they need.

- Inaccuracies may arise because of the design of the questionnaires or because trainees feel aggrieved and respond in different ways.

We therefore do need to look at evaluation in different ways, and certainly beyond the 'happiness sheet' approach. We certainly need to look at the total value of a learning event and not just how far it has achieved its objectives (Table 6.3).

Hamblin's model of evaluation as described by Reid and Barrington (1994) is helpful because it suggests methods at each level of the evaluation (Table 6.4).

Skills tips

- *Performance = ability × motivation*
  - If motivation is at an optimum, then to improve performance it is necessary to increase ability. This means further learning, which can be accomplished through training.

Table 6.3   Key evaluation questions

Why is the evaluation to be done?	For example, measure the impact of the event on individual performance; measure the impact on the survival of the organisation; justify the cost; establish effects on learners; improve the trainers.
What is to be evaluated?	The *CIRO* factors (Warr et al., 1970) *Context* within which the learning event has taken place: e.g., how accurately were needs diagnosed?; was the learning event appropriate?; what objectives were set? *Inputs* to the learning event: e.g. resources available and those actually used; media and methods used; validity of selection of learners. *Reactions* to the event by the various people involved in it. *Outcomes* of the event: e.g. the effects of the event in relation to the learning objectives set and those actually achieved.
How will the evaluation be done?	Depends on what is being evaluated (see above).
Who will do the evaluation?	Trainer, course designer, line manager, personnel manager, external consultant.
When will the evaluation be done?	Ideally before, during, at the immediate end, some time after and a longer time after. In practice it depends on what is to be evaluated and the purpose of the evaluation.

- If ability is constant and motivation poor, then it is necessary to increase motivation to improve performance.

- If ability needs to be increased to accommodate new changes, then it may well be that motivation needs to be increased to gain acceptance of the changes. This will again lead to improved performance.

Which all together means that you cannot successfully train people if they are not motivated. Conclusion: work on the motivation as well as the training (often a lot harder!).

Table 6.4   Hamblin's evaluation levels

The levels	Methods of evaluation
Level 1 Reactions of the trainees to the content and methods of training, to the trainer, and to other relevant factors What the trainee thought about the training	Discussion Interviews Questionnaires Recommendations of the trainees Desire for further training
Level 2 Learning attained during the learning period Did the trainees learn what was intended?	Objectives attained (Behaviour) Examinations, tests (Knowledge and understanding) Observation of demonstrated skills applied (Skills analysis) Projects or assignments (Skills analysis) Questionnaires (Attitude)
Level 3 Job behaviour in the work environment at the end of the training period Did the learning get transferred to the job?	Production rate Customer complaints Discussions with managers/subordinates/peers Activity sampling Self recording of specific incidents Evidence of competence Appraisal
Level 4 Effect on the department Has the training helped the department's performance?	Minutes of meetings Deadlines met Stress indicators Quality indicators Interview other managers/superiors
Level 5 The ultimate level Has the training affected the ultimate wellbeing of the organisation in terms of business objectives?	Growth Quality indicators Stress indicators Achievement of business goals and targets Standing of the training manager

- *Buddies*: Don't forget to use the expertise of others. This method is good for their self-esteem and more effective than most methods. Buddies are not just for new employees; they can work well for all experiences.

- *Coaching*: If everybody in your department was a good coach, work life would be a lot easier. Invest in coaching skills training for all and make the most of in-house talents.

Scaffolding summary

- Yet again, start with the strategy because any development must support overall business goals.
- Check out your learning climate – a poor one will make any learning difficult.
- Work out what development you think people need and have a plan (preferably on the wall).
- Identify needs at three levels: organisational, department and individual.
- Is training really the answer?
- Analyse the task, then analyse performance. Pinpoint the development gap.
- Decide how you are going to evaluate success in advance. Think big and go for good data – it will be easier to persuade senior management to spend more money in the future if you have hard results.
- Get people to self-assess their KSAs before and after.
- Continuous professional development is for all of us.

7

Review the structure

This is the simplest chapter of the lot. There are no complexities or tricks to reviewing the scaffolding, it's simply a case of revisiting everything you do on an annual basis to check that the whole structure is working effectively. If it isn't, change it.

The golden truths

- Ask your people and listen to what they say. Some people make constructive criticisms, but express themselves badly. Some people do not want to do things because they don't see the point. Explain it again.

- So, something is difficult to do. Well that does not mean it's not worth doing. Bad managers miss out the difficult bits.

- Audit some processes properly with a questionnaire for the participants or by gathering data from wherever you can. Get the facts and the statistics. An appraisal process, for example, can easily be audited with simple questionnaires for the reviewers and the reviewees.

- Try drawing a map of all the processes and their aims. Are you duplicating unnecessarily? Are there any gaps?

- Leave the scaffolding in place for a decent length of time before you change it. We all need to get used to new ways of working and how to behave with them. Some people take longer than others to get on board. Some processes suit long-term tenacity.

- Minor tweaks can be done at anytime, but stick to your core principles. Don't chuck the baby out with the bath water.

Audit yourself

McHale (1994) designed a useful tool to survey your team's perceptions of the way you manage and compare their views directly with yours; a sort of early, but simple 360-degree review. This team effectiveness survey can be very revealing, if you are up for it. The idea is that you mark yourself on the team leader's version, then hand out the other version to each person in your team to gather their perceptions of how you manage.

This activity needs positioning carefully with the team:

- Get them together and tell them you want their perceptions of you. This is your way of auditing yourself, no other reason at all. (Some people may be suspicious and jump to daft conclusions, maybe thinking it's a test for them).

- Tell them this eyeball to eyeball. One manager I know issued it by e-mail and caused more trouble than it was worth because most people did not understand what it was for, and thought the worst.

- Tell them it must be anonymous. Arrange for the completed surveys to be collected by a neutral person. No names, no pack drill.

- Collate the surveys yourself. Then you can see if you have just one or two people thinking differently to the rest.

- Ask yourself why the 'oddities' think that way. Is it them or is it you to blame? What can you do about it?

- You might be better than you thought. You might be worse. Whatever, think it through and plan positive actions.

- Get back to your team and tell them what you are going to do. They deserve an answer, whatever the result. If you leave it and don't regroup with them they will be let down.

One of my clients said to me 'I'm fine now, I have made a lot of progress since the CEO appraised me. There's only one person on my team who doesn't fit in'.

'Okay' I said. 'How about carrying out this survey then? It will prove to you and your CEO that you really have made progress' (the CEO still did not believe him).

So he did, bless his cotton socks, and the results were dreadful. He thought he was good and most of his team thought he was awful. Back to the drawing board for him and the start of some expensive coaching from me!

Most managers, though, just find one or two areas to work on, which seems to be the norm for all of us. Some are even pleasantly surprised, having got a bit stressed with all the scaffolding they lacked the confidence to believe how good they really were.

Panel 7.1 presents the questionnaire for managers/team leaders, and shows a list of items that describe how things might be in your team.

Please note that all the items are phrased positively; so think carefully about how true each one *really* is in the context of your team. Be honest and realistic. Tell them that there's nothing to be gained from taking too rosy a view of your team.

Panel 7.1: Team effectiveness questionnaire for managers/team leaders

Rating scale

1 = This statement is almost always true. It's a very accurate reflection of how things are here.

2 = This statement is true more often than not. It's a reasonably accurate reflection of how things are here.

3 = This statement is not true as often as it is true.

4 = More often than not, this statement is untrue. It reflects how things are here on some occasions only.

5 = This statement is rarely true. It is a very inaccurate reflection of how things are here.

1. Decision making	*1*	*2*	*3*	*4*	*5*
1. I very rarely, if ever, impose anything on my team.					
2. I discuss issues with the team, and jointly we agree what should be done.					
3. The team members and I jointly assess the effectiveness of the team.					
4. The team members and I jointly set the targets of the team.					
5. The way team members behave towards each other has been discussed and agreed by them; it is not something that I control.					

Panel 7.1: Team effectiveness questionnaire for managers/team leaders (*cont'd*)

2. Communication	1	2	3	4	5
6. Team members feel relaxed about discussing work with me.					
7. It's part of the team ethos that we all give each other open and honest feedback.					
8. Our feedback to each other is given as soon as possible after the event it describes; we do not wait for formal meetings to bring matters up.					
9. Our feedback is specific and constructive.					
10. I share my information freely with the team.					
3. Trust and valuing	1	2	3	4	5
11. I make it known that I recognise the value of each person's contribution					
12. I trust the team to act wisely in my absence.					
13. I don't feel the need to monitor and approve everything the team does.					
14. Team members are open with me and their colleagues about reporting failures as well as successes.					

Panel 7.1: Team effectiveness questionnaire for managers/team leaders (*cont'd*)

4. Objectives	1	2	3	4	5
15. The team knows exactly what they're aiming for.					
16. Objectives are discussed and agreed by the whole team; they are not something that I impose.					
17. The team get regular feedback on whether they are meeting their targets.					
18. Team member monitor themselves.					

5. Involvement	1	2	3	4	5
19. Each member of the team feels involved in the team's output.					
20. Members of the team frequently make suggestions about improving the way team works.					
21. I help them to work out the implications of their suggestions.					
22. I support the implementation of their suggestions.					
23. Each member feels they have an influence on what the team does.					

6. Team spirit	1	2	3	4	5
24. Team members collaborate with each other whenever possible.					

Panel 7.1: Team effectiveness questionnaire for managers/team leaders (*cont'd*)					
6. Team spirit	*1*	*2*	*3*	*4*	*5*
25. Team members share information and help each other.					
26. We all talk in terms of 'we' rather than 'I'.					
27. We all show we respect each other by avoiding put-downs and negative reactions to each other's suggestions.					
7. Performance	*1*	*2*	*3*	*4*	*5*
28. I am aware of the different strengths and weaknesses of the team.					
29. I take account of these differences when discussing work allocation with them.					
30. I adopt a coaching role towards team members.					

Panel 7.2 presents a similar questionnaire for team members. Items should be rated according to the five-point scale described in the panels.

Please note that all the items are phrased positively; so think carefully about how true each one *really* is in the context of your team. Be honest and realistic. Tell them that there's nothing to be gained from taking too rosy a view of your team.

Panel 7.2: Team effectiveness questionnaire for team members

Rating scale

1 = This statement is almost always true. It's a very accurate reflection of how things are here.

2 = This statement is true more often than not. It's a reasonably accurate reflection of how things are here.

3 = This statement is not true as often as it is true.

4 = More often than not, this statement is untrue. It reflects how things are here on some occasions only.

5 = This statement is rarely true. It is a very inaccurate reflection of how things are here.

1. Decision making	1	2	3	4	5
1. My manager very rarely, if ever, imposes anything on our team.					
2. He/she discusses issues with the team, and we jointly agree what should be done.					
3. The team members and the manager jointly assess the effectiveness of the team.					
4. The team members and the manager jointly set the targets of the team.					
5. We discuss and agree the way team members behave towards each other; it is not something that the manager controls.					

Panel 7.2: Team effectiveness questionnaire for team members (*cont'd*)

2. *Communication*	1	2	3	4	5
6. We feel relaxed about discussing work with the manager.					
7. It's part of the team ethos that we all give each other open and honest feedback.					
8. Our feedback to each other is given as soon as possible after the event it describes; we do not wait for formal meetings to bring matters up.					
9. Our feedback is specific and constructive.					
10. My manager shares his/her information freely with us.					

3. *Trust and valuing*	1	2	3	4	5
11. My manager makes it known that he/she recognises the value of each person's contribution.					
12. My manager trusts the team to act wisely in his/her absence.					
13. My manager does not feel the need to monitor and approve everything we do.					
14. We are open with the manager and our colleagues about reporting failures as well as successes.					

Panel 7.2: Team effectiveness questionnaire for team members (*cont'd*)

4. Objectives	1	2	3	4	5
15. We know exactly what we are aiming for.					
16. Objectives are discussed and agreed by the whole team; they are not something imposed by the manager.					
17. We get regular feedback on whether we are meeting our targets.					
18. We monitor ourselves.					
5. Involvement	1	2	3	4	5
19. Each member of the team feels involved in the team's output.					
20. We frequently make suggestions about improving the way the team works.					
21. My manager helps us to work out the implications of our suggestions.					
22. My manager supports the implementation of our suggestions.					
23. We feel that we have an influence on what the team does.					
6. Team spirit	1	2	3	4	5
24. We collaborate with each other whenever possible.					
25. We share information and help each other.					

Panel 7.2: Team effectiveness questionnaire for team members (*cont'd*)					
6. *Team spirit*	**1**	**2**	**3**	**4**	**5**
26. We all talk in terms of 'we' rather than 'I'.					
27. We all show we respect to each other by avoiding put-downs and negative reactions to each other's suggestions.					
7. *Performance*	**1**	**2**	**3**	**4**	**5**
28. My manager is aware of the different strengths and weaknesses of each one of us.					
29. The manager takes account of these differences when discussing work allocation with us.					
30. The manager adopts a coaching role towards us.					

Final skills tips

- When I was a very young manager I had an MD who would ask an incisive question when he was MBWA. I would answer and he would look at me calmly in silence. I would then add a bit more, then waffle, then start digging my pit even deeper. The tip therefore is, answer the question, state the facts and then shut up.

- Turning that one on its head, try it yourself on other people. They may not have learned to shut up, and then you get to find out all sorts of truths. If they do answer and keep quiet then it's brownie points for them. Maybe a good person to have by your side in a tricky situation.

- Play the game. There are certain issues that senior managers become fixated on. Unless you think they are proposing a major conflict with your beliefs go with it. More than that, be positive. You can always be constructively critical as you go along but if you start negatively you will be seen as the enemy.

The following tips come from an article written by Professor Thomas Kempner, Emeritus Professor of the Henley Management College and of Brunel University. Before that he was the Chairman of two medium-sized companies for over 20 years.

He knows that, if we are realistic, most of us managers know that we are likely to go on being subordinates for many years. Even if we get near to the top, we will always have to answer to at least one boss. Here is his advice to middle managers, based on what he would hope for in the good (absolutely perfect) subordinate:

1. *No nasty surprises.* I should never have to say 'You should have told me this before'.

2. *If you see a problem that may be beyond your level speak up.* Don't cover up until it's necessary to fire fight.

3. *Don't ask for immediate decisions.* You should have prepared the ground weeks ago.

4. *See your job in the context of the whole business.* You will be judged on your ability to see the whole picture and that may require sacrifices from your corner.

5. *Don't send me copies of memos that show how clever you have been.*

6. *Prepare your case carefully before we meet.*

7. *If you want an answer to a complex issue let me have the details in advance.* It's unreasonable to expect an instant reply on difficult issues.

8. *Press your views hard.* But once the decision is made carry it out as though it is your own.

9. *Don't whine.*

10. *Be brief.* I have a lot of other problems so try not to be one of them.

The final, final skills tip

You are trying to get buy-in from your team on a bit of scaffolding but it's like wading through treacle. You have done all the positioning, persuading and big picture stuff. Still they look at you with suspicion. Just say, 'Look I've just read a book on leadership. Humour me. We can always have an inquest afterwards'.

Bibliography

ACAS Code of Practice (2004) *Disciplinary and Grievance Procedure*. London: ACAS.

Armstrong, M. and Baron, A. (1995) *The Job Evaluation Handbook*. London: IPD.

Armstrong, M. and Baron, A. (2004) *Managing Performance*. London: CIPD.

Association for Information Management (ASLIB) *www.aslib.co.uk* (Accessed: 18 March 2005).

Barrington, H. and Reid, M. A. (1994) *Training Interventions*, 4th Edition, London: IPD.

Boydell, T. H. (1983) *A Guide to the Identification of Training Needs*. London: British Association for Commercial and Industrial Education, London.

Boydell, T. H. (1977) *A Guide to Job Analysis*. London: British Association for Commercial and Industrial Education.

Carroll, L. (1866) *Alice's Adventures in Wonderland*. New York: Harper Collins.

CRC Cambridge Regional College (2005) *Certificate in Personnel Practice Course Notes Handout*.

Davidson, H. (2002) *The Committed Enterprise: How to Make Vision and Values Work*. London: Butterworth Heinemann.

Drucker, P. (1958) *The Practice of Management*. London: Heinemann.

Easterby-Smith, M. and Tanton, M. (1985) 'Turning course evaluation from an end to a means'. *Personnel Management Magazine*, April.

Hackett, P. (1978) *Interview Skills Training: Role Play Exercises*. London: IPM.

Icke, A. (2003) *8-stage Communication Circle*. Unpublished, h2m Ltd.

Janis, L. and Mann, L. (1977) *Decision Making: Psychological Analysis of Conflict, Choice and Commitment*. New York: New York Free Press.

Kaplan, R. and Norton, D. (1996) *The Balanced Scorecard: Translating Strategy into Action*. Boston: Harvard Business School Press.

Kempner, T. (1990) 'Basic rules for pleasing the boss', *Sunday Times*, 23 September.

Lucey, T. (1997) *Management Information Systems*. 7th edition. London: Letts

Macdonald, J. (1999) *Knowledge Management in a Week*. London: Institute of Management.

Maier, N. (1958) *The Appraisal Interview: Objectives, Methods and Skills*. New York: John Wiley.

Marchand, D. and Davenport, T. (2000) *Mastering Information Management*. London: Financial Times, Prentice Hall.

McHale, J. (1994) Team Leading (Training video and book). London: BBC Worldwide Ltd.

MSA 'Interactive 360 feedback tool'. *www.msainteractive.com* (Accessed: 18 May 2005).

Oncken, W. and Wass, D. (1974) 'Management time: who's got the monkey', *Harvard Business Review*, Nov/Dec.

Peters, T., Waterman, R. and Philips J. (1980) 'Structure is not organisation', *Business Horizons*, 23 June.

Peters, T. and Waterman, R. (1982) *In Search of Excellence*. New York, London: Harper & Row.

Smith, M. and Robertson, I. T. (1986) *The Theory and the Practice of Systematic Staff Selection*. London: Macmillan.

Stoner, J. (1961) A Comparison of Individual and Group Decisions Involving Risk (Unpublished thesis MIT School of Industrial Management).

Torrington, D. and Hall, L. (1991) *Personnel Management: A New Approach*. 2nd Edition: Prentice Hall.

Venkatraman, N. (1996) *DIKAR Model*, The Value Centre, presentation made at Cranfield School of Management.

Wright, V. and Barding, L. (1992) 'A balanced performance', *Total Quality Magazine*.

Index

accountabilities, 10–12
  headings for, 57
action plans, agreeing and monitoring,
    108
analysis:
  quick, 8–10
  task, 121–2
  training needs, 118–21
  types of, 121
appraisal process, 105–6

background information required,
    19–20
behaviour management, skills tips,
    84–6
bigger picture plan, 65–6
business plan for department,
    template, 21
business plan, create your own, 18–23

communication circle, 38

data, assessing, 99–101
decision making, influencing outcome,
    87–8
develop, help people, 112
DIKAR model, 44

feedback, providing, 101–9
four-strategy pillar, 30

glue, 28, 48–51

induction, 76
information and knowledge
    management, what is, 43–4
information flow, 27, 38–72
information management, importance
    of, 44–5
information processes, 25–6

initiative, levels of, 57–9
interview:
  strategies, 71–3
  structure, 73–6
  structure, recommended pattern, 75
involvement and empowerment, 86–7

job description, 67–9
job role:
  accountabilities, 55–9
  understanding, 67–9
job, quoting for, 1–24

knowledge management, 27, 43–6

McKinsey 7-s, 5–7, 12, 13, 58
measures, writing, 63
meeting structure, 83
meetings:
  and recognition, 79–96
  basic rule, 79–80
  one-to-one, 80–1
  skills tips, 83–4
  team, 81–2
methods, 20–3
microstrategies, your department, 27,
    34
microstrategy, 28–34
monitoring work, 97–9

networking, 28, 46–8

objective setting process, 60–3
  basic steps, 56–7
objectives, agreeing, 59–63

performance management cycle, 55, 107
performance measurements, 32–4, 61–3
performance reviews, 103–4
  general view, 105

performance standards, setting, 63–4
PESTLE, 8
pick 'n' mix recognition actions, 91–5
plan, team and individual, 117
plan, traffic light, 35–6
plans, operational, 27, 34–7
positive action, 16–18
possible models, 12–14
processes, reporting, 39–41
progress, monitor and review people, 97–112
purpose, defining, 2–8
pyramid strategy model, 29

recognition, 88–9
recruitment process, 65–78
resources, providing, 64
reward, 88–9
reward realities, living with, 89–91

scaffolders, the, 53–79
scaffolding:
    is mine joined up?, 49–51
    step-by-step plan, 27–32
selection criteria, develop, 69

selection methods, 69–71
short-listing matrix with weighting, 70
simple strategy, template, 31
SMART objectives, 31, 60–1
styles, review, 106
SWOT, 8–10

table, questions to ask, 6
two-way mechanism, 41–2

underperformance:
    causes of, 110
    dealing with, 109–12
    six-step plan, 110

values, 14–18
vision, defining, 2–8
visually mapping network links, 48

what does the team think?, 14–15
where to collect data and for what table, 119
workforce chart, why develop, 115
workforce, why develop, 114–17